CONTENTS

LiverpoolFC · @liverpoolfc · @LFC · @liverpoolfc · @liverpoolfc

Published by Reach Sport · **Editor** William Hughes · **Writer** Chris McLoughlin · **Production Editors** Michael McGuinness, Roy Gilfoyle · **Design** Colin Sumpter, Adam Ward, Jonah Webb, Nick Loughlin · **Photography** Getty Images, Alamy, Liverpool Echo, John Powell, Andrew Powell, Nicholas Taylor, Nikki Dyer © Liverpool Football Club & Athletic Grounds Ltd ·
Marketing & Communications Manager Claire Brown · **Printed by** Buxton Press

IPSWICH TOWN FC 0
LIVERPOOL FC 2

Goals: Jota (60), Salah (65)
17.08.24 · Portman Road
Attendance: 30,014
Referee: Tim Robinson

IPSWICH TOWN FC (4-2-3-1): Walton, Tuanzebe (Szmodics 74), Woolfenden, Greaves, Davis, Morsy (C), Luongo (Taylor 65), Burns (Johnson 57), Chaplin (Harness 65), Hutchinson, Delap (Al-Hamadi 74). Subs not used: Slicker, Burgess, Phillips, Townsend. Booked: Woolfenden, Hutchinson, Burns.

LIVERPOOL FC (4-2-3-1): Alisson, Alexander-Arnold (Bradley 77), Quansah (Konate 46), Van Dijk (C), Robertson (Tsimikas 79), Gravenberch, Mac Allister, Salah, Szoboszlai, Diaz, Jota (Gakpo 79). Subs not used: Kelleher, Endo, Nunez, Jones, Elliott. Booked: Gakpo.

PRESS BOX:
JOHN BREWIN, THE OBSERVER
"Jarell Quansah was replaced by Ibrahima Konate at the break. A tactical decision, confirmed Slot, a quiet touchline presence compared to his predecessor, more darts player stalking the oche than ants-in-pants berserker. He had, though, made himself heard. The passing was crisper, the pressing far more aggressive. Liverpool chances finally arrived."

PUNDIT:
PETER CROUCH, TNT SPORTS
"Liverpool needed to make a statement with the new manager and no signings. Some of the ways they opened Ipswich up, they looked like they were going to score at will. There are slight differences between Slot and Klopp but the fans will get on board."

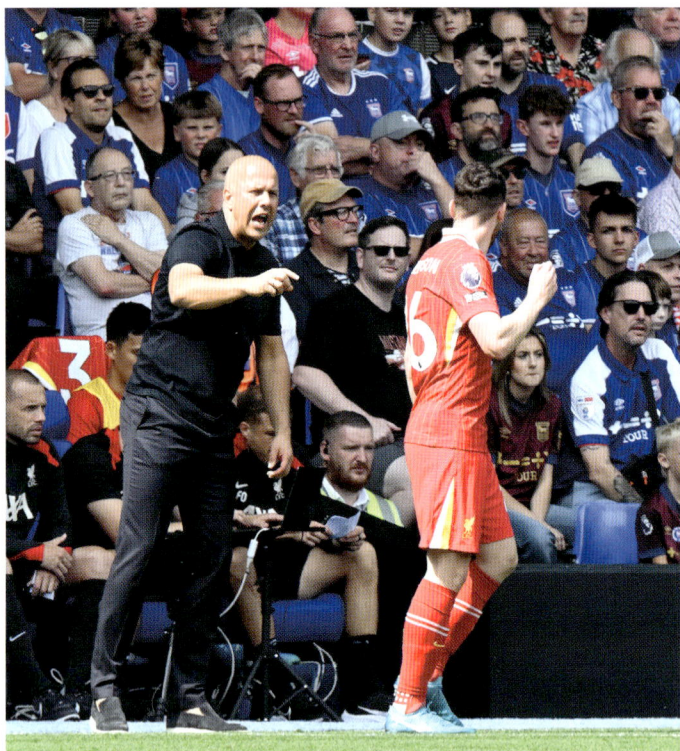

HEAD COACH: ARNE SLOT

"We as a team made a big change at half-time because we came out totally different to how we had come out in the first half. Second half, we won more duels, we won more second balls and we played more balls in behind because if the other team takes the risk of playing one-v-one and you have the likes of Luis Diaz, Mo Salah and Diogo Jota then use them, play the balls in behind. That's what we did better in the second half and from there gaps opened up and you could see how good and how well we could play in possession."

FOR THE RECORD:

Mo Salah became the first player in Premier League history to score nine goals in total on the opening weekend of the season.

ALSO THIS WEEKEND: Everton 0-3 Brighton & Hove Albion
Chelsea 0-2 Manchester City
Arsenal 2-0 Wolverhampton Wanderers

REPORT:

Arne Slot arrived at Portman Road with history against him. Not since 1991 had a new Liverpool FC manager won his first league game.

That happened to be Graeme Souness, against Ipswich Town's East Anglian rivals Norwich City, but at Anfield. The last Reds boss to win his first league game away from home was Bob Paisley, at Luton Town, all the way back in 1974.

So with most people predicting a year of transition for the Reds as Slot began the seemingly impossible job of following Jürgen Klopp, and the newly-promoted Tractor Boys desperate to make hay in the Premier League after 22 years away, there was talk that Liverpool could come a cropper.

Yet history has a funny way of repeating itself at LFC.

Back in '74, many thought following the great Bill Shankly was an impossible job for Paisley, but he gradually put his own stamp on Shankly's team and guided Liverpool to unprecedented glory.

So while there may have been a new head coach and coaching staff on the Liverpool bench in Suffolk, the 11 players and nine substitutes Slot named for his first game had all played under his predecessor. Continuity always was a Liverpool watchword.

Klopp, it was well established, was no fan of 12.30pm Saturday kick-offs, but while TNT Sports may have been hoping for David to bring down Goliath in the cornfield, the former Feyenoord boss gave a shrewd pre-match assessment.

"If 12.30 was a difficult time to perform, then I'm a really stupid manager because we train every day at 12 o'clock," he said with a smile. "I don't think it has so much to do with the 12.30 kick-offs, for me, it is that every away game is difficult. I showed them last week that 10 out of 18 away games last season didn't lead to a win. You can then argue if it is 12.30 or is it just difficult to play an away game."

While Ipswich's minority shareholder and shirt sponsor Ed Sheeran is in love with the Shape of You, it was the shape of Slot's first starting XI that truly ushered in the new era. Out went Klopp's 4-3-3, in came Slot's 4-2-3-1 with Ryan Gravenberch playing as a no6 alongside Alexis Mac Allister, Dominik Szoboszlai operating behind Diogo Jota with Mo Salah and Luis Diaz out wide.

In a free-kick-riddled first half it took time for the Reds to settle. Alisson was forced to keep out a Jacob Greaves header and an Omari Hutchison shot in the opening 32 minutes before the already-booked Wes Burns conceded a free-kick for deliberate handball before kicking the ball away. Referee Tim Robinson generously didn't dismiss him.

Slot used the half-time interval to change things. Jarell Quansah was replaced by Ibrahima Konate at half-time and the Reds came out with renewed attacking zest.

Salah had a shot blocked before a slick attack ended with Diaz deftly dinking Trent Alexander-Arnold's pass over Ipswich goalie Christian Walton, but also the crossbar. Szoboszlai and Mac Allister also had efforts blocked before the unmarked Jota met Alexander-Arnold's cross six yards out, but glanced the ball wide.

Alexander-Arnold's influence was growing and his beautifully-guided pass sent Salah running down the wing on the hour mark. He squared the ball for Jota the slotter, who netted Liverpool's first goal under Slot.

The travelling Kop only had a five-minute wait for the next one. Salah controlled a glorious diagonal pass from Virgil van Dijk and played a one-two with Szoboszlai. Town left-back Lief Davis tried to intercept, but toed the ball into Salah's path and for the seventh time in eight seasons Mo had an opening-day goal.

He marked the occasion with a UFC-inspired archery celebration and could have been reaching for the bow and arrow again only for Walton to palm out his volley before substitute Conor Bradley had a shot from the rebound blocked.

Walton also saved from Bradley with the Reds looking like they'd score every time they went forward, but 2-0 was enough to condemn Ipswich to a first home defeat in almost a year.

When Liverpool last won the Premier League in 2019/20 the season began with a victory against an East Anglian side with Salah on the scoresheet.

Maybe history isn't against Arne Slot after all.

LIVERPOOL FC 2
BRENTFORD FC 0

Goals: Diaz (13), Salah (70)

25.08.24 · Anfield · Attendance: 60,107

Referee: Stuart Attwell

LIVERPOOL (4-2-3-1): Alisson, Alexander-Arnold (Bradley 72), Konate, Van Dijk (C), Robertson, Gravenberch (Endo 90+1), Mac Allister, Salah (Elliott 83), Szoboszlai, Diaz (Gakpo 72), Jota (Nunez 72). Subs not used: Kelleher, Gomez, Tsimikas, Quansah. Booked: Szoboszlai, Gravenberch.

BRENTFORD (4-4-2): Flekken, Roerslev, Collins, Pinnock, Ajer, Jensen (Carvalho 66), Norgaard (C), Janelt (Onyeka 73), Lewis-Potter (Damsgaard 66), Mbeumo, Wissa (Schade 73). Subs not used: Valdimarsson, Mee, Trevitt, Yarmoliuk, Van den Berg. Booked: Nørgaard, Jensen, Mbeumo.

PRESS BOX:

GREGG EVANS, THE ATHLETIC

"Slot has told his players to make 'every pass count' and when Liverpool pushed Brentford back and dominated possession they played some of their best stuff, much to the delight of the home crowd who chanted the head coach's name on 82 minutes. The biggest takeaway, though, was how at ease Liverpool look under their new manager – and how ready the supporters are to go with him as he builds his post-Klopp team."

PUNDIT:

JAMIE CARRAGHER, SKY SPORTS

"Last season was a rollercoaster ride for supporters; late goals, coming from behind. It felt like every game was like a cup final. Liverpool needed more games like this last season. That was almost like a Man City performance in that the game felt over when the second goal went in. There wasn't any jeopardy in the game."

REPORT:

The last time Liverpool supporters saw their manager at Anfield for a Premier League match he was chanting the name of Arne Slot down a microphone on the pitch.

Three months after Jürgen Klopp got the chant going, the Kop could serenade the Dutchman in person, and did so with another three points in the bag. Slot had already received an Anfield welcome for the pre-season friendly against Sevilla and was keen to play down his competitive home debut as Reds boss.

"I do not want to dwell too much on the fact that this will be my first competitive fixture at Anfield in my new role as head coach," he wrote in the Matchday Programme. "It goes without saying that this is a big honour for me and also for my staff, but at the same time our only focus will be on the game itself."

So when the 45-year-old emerged from the Anfield tunnel before kick-off, with a raincoat draped over his arm in preparation for the traditional August weather, it was with no fanfare.

He gave a little wave to the Main Stand and Kop and, with a banner behind him that read 'From Bergentheim to Anfield, We've Got Your Back Arne', took his place on the home bench. He was soon back on his feet to give those who had made it a big smile and thumbs-up, but then all attention turned to Thomas Frank's Brentford.

The Bees are a modern, classier reincarnation of 1980s Wimbledon. Physically strong, they challenge for everything, cross balls at every opportunity and do mad things from set-pieces, such as pack the six-yard box so densely it's like a Lime Street Station platform at rush hour.

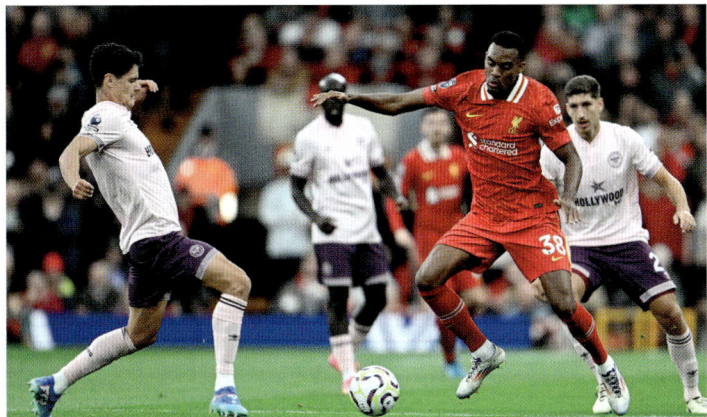

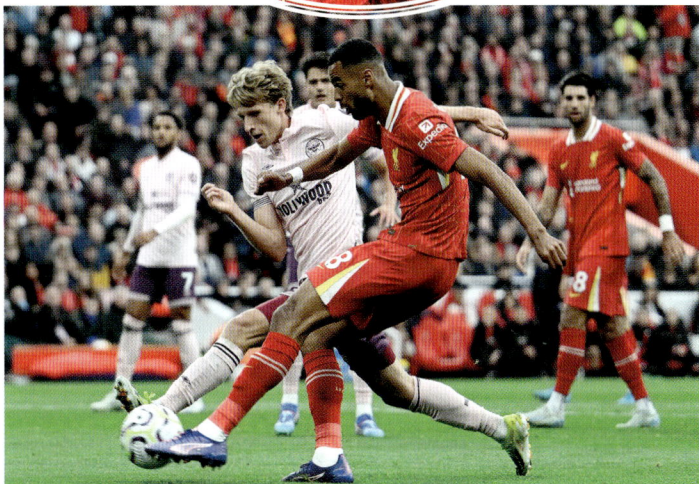

HEAD COACH: ARNE SLOT

"The reception of the fans was similar to the reception I got from all the people in and around the AXA [Training Centre] and the people who are working for Liverpool. So, I think I cannot speak for all of the managers, but I think maybe all of them would tell you the same: every manager that comes in here feels the warmth of this club, feels the appreciation of the fans, and the most important thing we have to do as managers is to make sure the team plays in a style that the fans like to see. That's what we are trying and I think the boys showed that, and the fans showed their appreciation for that, I think."

FOR THE RECORD:

The attendance of 60,107 was a new Anfield league record.

ALSO THIS WEEKEND:

Brighton & Hove Albion 2-1 Manchester United
Tottenham Hotspur 4-0 Everton
Aston Villa 0-2 Arsenal

But in Mikkel Damsgaard and Bryan Mbeumo they also have quality, making Brentford opponents perhaps unlike any other Slot had faced in his managerial career at AZ and Feyenoord. To beat them, you need control.

Slot had spoken about taking Klopp's 'Liverpool 2.0' of last season and refining it. Whereas there was always a bit of chaos about Jürgen's hugely enjoyable and successful style of football, Slot's tactical ethos is more controlled, more structured.

It was evident for the first time at Anfield against a Brentford side that were limited to just 10 touches in the Liverpool penalty area and two shots on target.

After a quiet opening 12 minutes the game burst into life from a Brentford corner. Mathias Jensen whipped it into the near post where

four visiting players had congregated like they were waiting at a bus stop in Hounslow, but it was Ibrahima Konate who soared highest to clear. Mo Salah won a challenge on the edge of the box and, all of a sudden, a two-v-two break was on.

Diogo Jota brought the ball forward and Luis Diaz cleverly made a diagonal run from right to left that allowed Jota to play him in. The Colombian outpaced Mbeumo, who was strangely the last man, and struck a rising, left-footed drive high into the net past Mark Flekken to have Anfield on its feet.

Controlling a game may be the foundation Slot's castle is built upon, but not at the cost of the explosive counter-attacks that Kopites have become so accustomed to. It showed that Slot's Liverpool aim to combine the best of both worlds.

Andy Robertson, from a Diaz pass, almost beat Flekken at his near post moments later before Christian Nørgaard wasted Brentford's best chance when he tried to glance home a dangerous Mbeumo free-kick, but missed the ball completely.

Flekken denied Robertson again early in the second half with a flying save, when the Scot headed Jota's overhead kick goalwards, and, in the 56th minute, Alisson made his only difficult save of the afternoon when he beat out a Nathan Collins header from another set-piece.

Trent Alexander-Arnold almost caught the Bees goalie out when he rattled the post directly from a corner and Flekken had to work overtime, diving to save a Konate header and fingertip a Diaz effort past the post.

A second goal felt inevitable and it was Salah, yet again, who got it. Diaz found him in space and he eased the ball beyond Flekken with a swish of his paintbrush of a left foot.

Cody Gakpo, on from the bench, also struck the crossbar with a shot that clipped the head of Collins on the way past Flekken, but Anfield had seen enough.

"Arne Slot, na na, nah na na," they chanted. Just like Klopp had.

MANCHESTER UNITED FC 0
LIVERPOOL FC 3

Goals: Diaz (35, 42), Salah (56)

01.09.24 · Old Trafford · Attendance: 73,738

Referee: Anthony Taylor

MANCHESTER UNITED (4-2-3-1): Onana, Mazraoui, De Ligt (Maguire 69), Martinez, Dalot, Casemiro (Collyer 46), Mainoo, Garnacho (Diallo 69), Fernandes (C), Rashford, Zirkzee (Eriksen 86). Subs not used: Bayindir, Heaton, Evans, Wheatley, Antony. Booked: Zirkzee, Martinez, Mainoo, De Ligt.

LIVERPOOL (4-2-3-1): Alisson, Alexander-Arnold (Bradley 76), Konate, Van Dijk, Robertson (Tsimikas 83), Gravenberch, Mac Allister, Salah, Szoboszlai, Diaz (Gakpo 66), Jota (Nunez 76). Subs not used: Kelleher, Gomez, Endo, Elliott, Quansah. Booked: Van Dijk.

PRESS BOX:
JASON BURT, DAILY TELEGRAPH
"It may not have been the 7-0 at Anfield in March 2023, or the 5-0 at Old Trafford in October 2021, but it felt like it such was the supremacy exerted by Liverpool. Arne Slot now has a perfect record of played three, won three, without conceding a goal. He also became the first Liverpool manager since George Kay in 1936 to win his first game at Old Trafford."

PUNDIT:
DION DUBLIN, BBC RADIO FIVE LIVE
"Slot hasn't tried to rewrite anything. He's made small tweaks. He's gone into Liverpool and tweaked it so they play how he wants. They look so smooth. They're not as explosive as they were under Jürgen Klopp, but it looks more organised. I thought Szoboszlai and Mac Allister were great, but Gravenberch was man of the match."

HEAD COACH: ARNE SLOT
"I think everything you want to see as a manager you saw in this game.

United started really well and we conceded one or two corner kicks in that moment. But we fought ourselves through those moments and then we got the disallowed goal, but there was no negative reaction at all. We just kept on playing afterwards: scoring three, we could have scored more, two important saves from Ali in the second half. So, everything was there and maybe the one that was most important is that the work-rate was incredible by all of them without the ball, and that makes it a very positive day today."

FOR THE RECORD:
Mo Salah became only the second Liverpool player to score 10+ goals at a venue other than Anfield after Ian Rush, who scored 13 at Goodison Park and 10 at Wembley.

ALSO THIS WEEKEND:
Arsenal 1-1 Brighton & Hove Albion
Newcastle United 2-1 Tottenham Hotspur
Everton 2-3 Bournemouth

REPORT:

As they slept the night before the biggest clash in English football, Manchester United fans would have been forgiven for waking up in cold sweat with Mo Salah on their minds.

The Egyptian went into this fixture having scored 14 goals in 15 appearances against United including 11 in the Premier League – the most in the competition's history – and a club/league record six at Old Trafford, including a hat-trick in a 5-0 win in 2021.

Salah also got two in Liverpool's 7-0 thrashing of their rivals at Anfield in 2023 and another goal in this game would make Old Trafford the first away stadium any Red had scored at in seven consecutive appearances.

So when his goal came the only surprise was that it took Salah 56 minutes, but in the meantime he clocked up two assists in a 3-0 victory that was utterly comprehensive.

Arne Slot had lost his last two matches against Erik ten Hag with his Feyenoord side, losing the most recent clash 3-2 to an Ajax team that had Ryan Gravenberch in it, but now the Dutch midfielder was his player and he ran the show at Old Trafford.

Gravenberch was so good that LFCTV released a video of his best clips and among them was a drop of the shoulder and driving run forward that left Kobbie Mainoo chasing his shadow. It led to a goal.

After reaching the edge of United's penalty area Gravenberch played the ball to Luis Diaz, who fired it across the six-yard box. Arriving at the far post was Trent Alexander-Arnold and although his shot was blocked by Diogo Dalot, a buzz of Anthony Taylor's watch signalled it had crossed the line.

Alexander-Arnold ran past the Stretford End and kissed the camera à la Steven Gerrard, but his smacker was replaced with a smack to the face. A VAR review concluded that Salah was in an offside position when Diaz crossed and the home fans cheered the goal being ruled out like their own team had scored.

It turned out to be the only thing they had to celebrate and after Casemiro got away with leaving stud marks on Alexis Mac Allister's stomach it was Liverpool who continued to dominate.

All that was missing was a goal and it arrived in the 35th minute when Gravenberch picked off a Casemiro pass, drove forward and found Salah in the penalty area.

He crossed to the far post where both Diaz and Dominik Szoboszlai were completely unmarked. Both jumped for the ball and for a second it appeared they would clatter into each other, but Szoboszlai shrewdly ducked after realising Diaz had a better run at the cross and from four yards out he headed past Andre Onana.

There was no VAR to come to United's rescue this time and although Alisson was finally called into action to save a Noussair Mazraoui shot, the second goal was only going to be scored by one team.

Casemiro dwelt in possession and Diaz chased back to nick the ball off his toe. Mac Allister gave Diaz the ball back, he slipped it out to Salah and ran into the penalty area to guide the return pass beyond Onana into the bottom corner. Two nil, and it all looked so easy.

Alisson had to dive to his left early in the second period to push away Joshua Zirkzee's shot, but Salah's traditional Old Trafford goal was due and soon arrived. Mac Allister won a tackle in midfield, Szoboszlai burst forward and Salah didn't even take a touch before sweeping the ball home and running to the merry men and women in the away end and breaking out his bow and arrow celebration once again.

United gave Salah an opportunity to make it 4-0 straight from the kick-off when Lisandro Martinez presented him with the ball, but he fired narrowly over after cutting inside. The travelling Kop even got the oles out as one quick-fire passing move resulted in Salah's curler deflecting narrowly wide and although Alisson made a great save from Zirkzee's header it was Szoboszlai who wasted the best chance to add another goal, taking too long before shooting.

It mattered not. Andy Robertson's 300th LFC appearance, Virgil van Dijk's 200th LFC league match and Diogo Jota's 100th LFC league game was already won and with that man Salah getting a goal and two assists, the red half of Manchester must have woken up the next morning hoping it was all a nightmare. Again.

MANCHESTER UNITED 0 | 17:55
LIVERPOOL 3 | 95:03

LIVERPOOL FC 0
NOTTINGHAM FOREST FC 1

Goal: Hudson-Odoi (72)

14.09.24 · Anfield · Attendance: 60,344

Referee: Michael Oliver

LIVERPOOL (4-2-3-1): Alisson, Alexander-Arnold, Konate (Jones 75), Van Dijk (C), Robertson (Tsimikas 75), Gravenberch, Mac Allister (Bradley 60), Salah, Szoboszlai, Diaz (Gakpo 61), Jota (Nunez 60). Subs not used: Kelleher, Gomez, Endo, Quansah. Booked: Robertson, Gravenberch, Szoboszlai, Alexander-Arnold.

NOTTINGHAM FOREST (4-2-3-1): Sels, Aina, Milenkovic, Murillo, Moreno (Williams 80), Yates (C), Ward-Prowse, Dominguez (Hudson-Odoi 54), Gibbs-White (Morato 81), Anderson (Elanga 61), Wood (Jota Silva 81). Subs not used: Miguel, Awoniyi, Omobamidele, Toffolo. Booked: Moreno, Yates, Sels, Elanga.

PRESS BOX:

LEWIS STEELE, DAILY MAIL

"Arne Slot's buzz word since taking over has been patience – but by around the 70th minute, any patience had been slowly strangled to submission and the overriding emotions were just angst and frustration. Even after they took the lead, Forest goalkeeper Matz Sels was barely called into action as a wasteful Liverpool continued to shoot from distance and were unable to break down the away team's sturdy rearguard."

PUNDIT:

RAY HOUGHTON, LFCTV

"We talked about coming out and being positive from the first whistle and taking the game to the opposition, I didn't see that today. I thought our passing was a bit slow, too slow at times. Liverpool can only look at themselves and the manager will learn a great deal. It's not always when winning that you learn a lot about your teams, it's when you lose as well. He will learn about players coming back from an international break."

REPORT:

A bump in the road or the first sign that Liverpool had made a false start under Arne Slot? The Reds' first home defeat to Nottingham Forest since 1969 was certainly a reality check.

Man hadn't landed on the moon when the visitors last won at Anfield and while it ultimately proved to be one small misstep for the Redmen, it was one giant leap for Forestkind.

After finishing 17th in 2023/24, six points above the drop zone, Nuno Espirito Santo's men arrived on Merseyside unbeaten with a win and two draws from their opening three games, but few people expected them to hand Slot a first defeat as Reds boss.

Not even Brian Clough had guided Forest to a win at Anfield when they were in their pomp, winning a First Division title and two European Cups in the late 1970s and early 1980s, but Liverpool's

28-game unbeaten home run against their visitors came to an end. It turned out to be evidence that Nottingham Forest were in for a successful season and a rare off-day for Liverpool. The Reds managed just five shots on target, which was two more than the Garibaldi, and it looked like a 0-0 draw waiting to happen until Callum Hudson-Odoi curled home a 72nd-minute winner.

The fact that it was Liverpool's first game under Slot following an international break became a talking point at full-time as some of his Reds looked a tad jaded, but sometimes you need a setback to learn lessons and improve.

Before kick-off, Kopites displayed a 'Rowdy 5' mosaic in memory of former skipper Ron Yeats, who had passed away eight days earlier at the age of 86. A special matchday programme cover and a minute's

HEAD COACH: ARNE SLOT

"We had a lot of ball possession but only managed to create three or four quite good chances, so that is by far not enough if you have so much ball possession. If you play so much in their half, we need to do much better. We lost the ball so many times in simple situations. That is, I think, the main story from the game: ball possession not good enough."

FOR THE RECORD:

This was the first time Liverpool had failed to score against Nottingham Forest at Anfield since a 0-0 draw in 1993.

ALSO THIS WEEKEND:

Tottenham Hotspur 0-1 Arsenal
Aston Villa 3-2 Everton
Manchester City 2-1 Brentford

applause were among the other tributes for a man who captained the Reds in 417 of his 454 appearances and got his hands on the FA Cup before any other Liverpool player.

Quite simply he was the colossus cornerstone of Bill Shankly's Anfield revolution.

After a quiet opening 16 minutes it was the persistence of Luis Diaz that led to the first chance of note. Ryan Gravenberch overhit a pass and looked away in disgust, but Diaz didn't write it off as a lost cause.

Ryan Yates ambled back, assuming the ball was going out for a goal kick, but Diaz chased him down, kept the ball in and left the Forest skipper on the deck in a panic, appealing for a free-kick.

Diaz had committed no offence and cut into the box before wrong-footing Forest keeper Matz Sels with a low shot that beat

him, but cannoned back out off the foot of the post. Moments later, Dominik Szoboszlai headed a Mo Salah cross wide of the target after Gravenberch led a counter-attack before Morgan Gibbs-White raced through and curled past the post, but a delayed offside flag would have ruled a goal out anyway.

Diogo Jota forced Sels into his first save of the afternoon when he connected with a lovely Alexis Mac Allister cross six yards from goal, but under a challenge from Alex Moreno he could only shin the ball straight into the goalkeeper's arms.

Trent Alexander-Arnold almost caught Sels out when he shot from a corner, the Forest keeper pushing the ball over, and he also had to dive full-stretch to his left to palm out a Mac Allister header from Alexander-Arnold's cross.

Sels almost spilled a looping Diaz header into his own net too, but managed to grab the ball before it crossed the goalline, much to his relief.

Salah also made the Belgian save at his near post after shooting from a tight angle early in the second half, but when Hudson-Odoi and Anthony Elanga came on from the bench Forest suddenly looked a serious threat on the counter-attack.

Elanga blazed a shot over and not long after Ola Aina cleared a deflected corner off the goalline, they took the lead. Darwin Nunez was tackled, Elanga burst forward and sprayed a pass out to Hudson-Odoi, who cut inside Conor Bradley and beat Alisson with a low curling shot from 20 yards.

Alisson prevented Elanga from making it 2-0 when he fired goalwards from a Chris Wood flick-on and, in truth, Forest held on to their lead comfortably.

The closest Liverpool came to equalising was a Szoboszlai shot that Murillo deflected narrowly wide.

After 55 years, Nottingham Forest finally had an Anfield victory while Liverpool had an early reality check under Slot, but how they responded would shape the season.

LIVERPOOL FC 3
AFC BOURNEMOUTH 0

Goals: Diaz (26, 28), Nunez (37)
21.09.24 · Anfield · Attendance: 60,347
Referee: Tony Harrington

LIVERPOOL (4-2-3-1): Kelleher, Alexander-Arnold, Konate, Van Dijk (C), Robertson, Gravenberch, Mac Allister, Salah, Szoboszlai (Jones 61), Diaz (Gakpo 72), Nunez (Chiesa 72). Subs not used: Jaros, Gomez, Jota, Tsimikas, Quansah, Bradley. Booked: Konate.

BOURNEMOUTH (4-2-3-1): Arrizabalaga, Araujo (Smith 69), Zabarnyi, Huijsen, Kerkez, Cook (C), Christie (Scott 69), Semenyo (Sinisterra 70), Kluivert (Ouattara 46), Tavernier, Evanilson (Unal 76). Subs not used: Travers, Senesi, Brooks, Hill. Booked: Christie, Kluivert, Iraola, Cook.

PRESS BOX:
JONATHAN NORCROFT, THE SUNDAY TIMES
"Darwin Nunez is like Forrest Gump's box of chocolates: you never know what you're gonna get. When the striker does unwrap a good one, it's delicious. His coruscating goal, curled home audaciously at the end of a sweeping break, had him crying tears of joy."

PUNDIT:
DANNY MURPHY, BBC MATCH OF THE DAY
"There is a very deliberate effort from Liverpool to play out slower and to control things a bit more under Slot, but there are also some similar things to Klopp such as the high press. The great thing today was balance. Bournemouth were brave and had a high line but the decision making on when to play short and when to play long was brilliant."

HEAD COACH: ARNE SLOT

"I learn from them day by day and I was curious to see how we would react after the Milan game. After the United game, which was a big win, or a statement win I think you call it in England, then to see us coming back against Nottingham Forest like that, that was not what you expect from a team that wants to compete for something. So, after the big win against AC Milan I was curious to see how we would react – and it was a much, much better reaction than we had against Nottingham Forest."

FOR THE RECORD:

Trent Alexander-Arnold's assist was his 81st for LFC and his 100th goal involvement, making him at 25 the youngest player to reach that milestone since Steven Gerrard in 2005.

ALSO THIS WEEKEND:

Manchester City 2-2 Arsenal
Aston Villa 3-1 Wolverhampton Wanderers
Fulham 3-1 Newcastle United

REPORT:

His name is Lucho. He came from Porto. He came to score, came to score, came to score, score, score.

When the Luis Diaz song, to the tune of Bella Ciao, was dreamt up by Liverpool supporters they didn't have Bournemouth in mind. But after this 3-0 victory you could be forgiven for thinking it was written in homage to the Barrancas-born forward's personal record against the Cherries.

Diaz's double took his tally to five goals in three Anfield appearances against Bournemouth. He came to score, came to score, came to score, score, score against them indeed.

The swivel-hipped Colombian bagged the first and last goals in a record 9-0 home win against Bournemouth in 2022 and followed it up with the opening goal in a 3-1 Anfield success in 2023, so nobody needed a lie down for shock when Diaz broke the deadlock in the 26th minute, albeit after an early scare.

Liverpool had responded to the home defeat to Nottingham Forest by beating AC Milan 2-1 in the San Siro to give birthday boy Arne Slot victory in his first Champions League match, but the Reds had again conceded first.

That trend looked like continuing in the fourth minute when Andoni Iraola's side launched a swift counter-attack that saw Justin Kluivert drive through the middle and strike a shot that Antoine Semenyo slid in to convert at the far post.

The flag stayed down, but VAR took a look and moments later referee Tony Harringon was drawing an imaginary rectangle in the air and chalking it off.

With the Anfield crowd lifted by the let-off the Reds cracked on and Andy Robertson slid Mo Salah's cross into the side-netting before Diaz forced Kepa Arrizabalaga into a flying tip over when he cut inside and unleashed a powerful shot from 20 yards out.

The Spaniard also had to dive to his left to deny Salah when he was picked out by an exquisite Alexis Mac Allister pass on the half-volley that deserved to be an assist.

At the other end, Caoimhin Kelleher – in for the injured Alisson – did well to save from Semenyo in a one-v-one after Evanilson had charged his attempted clearance down, but it was Diaz who looked constantly dangerous.

In the 24th minute he showed skill to cut between two Bournemouth defenders and pace to burst into the box, but couldn't beat Kepa. It was a different story moments later.

The Reds had been building from the back, but Ibrahima Konate spotted Diaz shaping to make a diagonal run and caught Bournemouth's high-line cold by playing a long ball forward.

Kepa spotted the danger and rushed out of his penalty area to intercept, but Diaz got there first, brought the ball down on his thigh and dribbled past the Bournemouth 'keeper before slotting past Julian Araujo, who'd raced back to cover.

Liverpool led 1-0 and like the no26 bus on Sheil Road, you wait 26 minutes for a Diaz goal and then two come along at once.

This time it was Trent Alexander-Arnold who received a Salah pass and raced down the right before guiding the ball across to Diaz, who controlled it with his right foot and slipped it underneath the diving Kepa with his left for a quick-fire double.

If Kopites thought that counter-attack was good, what happened in the 37th minute was even better. Darwin Nunez headed Konate's chipped pass towards Salah and darted forward for the Egyptian to play him in down the right with one touch. Nunez ran at Illya Zabarnyi, cut inside onto his left foot and curled a gorgeous shot goalwards that beat Kepa and glanced the inside of the far post on the way in.

Salah missed a chance to make it 4-0 before the break, Milos Kerkez blocked another Salah effort on the line and Kepa denied him again as the Reds continued to create chances, not least when Federico Chiesa came on for his home debut.

Seconds after replacing Nunez, the ball dropped invitingly for the Italian, from Cody Gakpo's flick-on, and with his first touch he blasted a half-volley from 25 yards out straight at Kepa.

Bournemouth almost got one back when Kelleher saved from Luis Sinisterra and the same player headed against the bar before the Liverpool goalie clawed the rebound off the line, but it was another Colombian everyone left Anfield talking about.

His name is Lucho.

WOLVERHAMPTON WANDERERS FC v LIVERPOOL FC

REPORT:

A little over 12 months ago, Ryan Gravenberch made his Liverpool debut at Molineux. Signed from Bayern Munich, the Dutch international midfielder came on as a 93rd-minute substitute for Mo Salah with the match already won.

It was the start of a stop-start campaign. Gravenberch made 38 appearances under Jürgen Klopp, but 17 of them came from the bench. He never started more than three consecutive games and only completed 90 minutes twice.

"To be honest, I like a period to adapt," he told WalkOn, the LFC Members magazine, ahead of the season. "I wasn't used to the Prem, of course, and I didn't play a lot of football before I came here, but I had the time to adapt and I really needed it. Now we've started on zero again with the new coach."

Six games is a little early to be booking the open-top bus, but Arne Slot's decision to switch Gravenberch from a no8 to a no6 looks like a stroke of genius. It later transpired that assistant coach Johnny Heitinga had been working closely with his fellow Dutchman.

The 22-year-old was the Reds' best player in this 2-1 victory at Wolves. He won every duel and tackle he competed for and, alongside Alexis Mac Allister, controlled the midfield on an evening when the Reds weren't quite at their attacking best, but took the three points required to leapfrog Arsenal at the top of the table.

Alisson was back in goal, minus his facial hair which had clearly had a date with a razor, but Darwin Nunez was ruled out through illness. Diogo Jota started upfront against his former club and it was the men in old gold who began the better. Jean-Ricner Bellegarde forced

WOLVERHAMPTON WANDERERS FC 1
LIVERPOOL FC 2

Goals: Konate (45+2), Ait-Nouri (56), Salah (61pen)

28.09.24 · Molineux · Attendance: 31,413
Referee: Anthony Taylor

LIVERPOOL (4-2-3-1): Alisson, Alexander-Arnold, Konate, Van Dijk (C), Robertson (Gomez 89), Gravenberch, Mac Allister, Salah, Szoboszlai (Jones 73), Diaz (Gakpo 73), Jota. Subs not used: Kelleher, Endo, Chiesa, Tsimikas, Bradley, Quansah. Booked: Alexander-Arnold, Jota, Hulshoff, Konate.

WOLVES (4-1-4-1): Johnstone, Semedo, Bueno (Doyle 77), T Gomes, Ait-Nouri, Andre, Cunha, Lemina (C), J Gomes, Bellegarde (Forbs 52), Larsen (Hwang 68). Subs not used: Sa, Doherty, R Gomes, Sarabia, Guedes, Pond. Booked: Andre, Derry, Forbs.

PRESS BOX:
JAMES PEARCE, THE ATHLETIC
"On a day when Liverpool never really clicked as an attacking force, Slot was again grateful for a dominant display from Ryan Gravenberch, who continues to shine in the holding midfield role."

PUNDIT:
OWEN HARGREAVES, PREMIER LEAGUE PRODUCTIONS
"Gravenberch is 190cm, he is 22 years old, he has got everything, but he is not a specialist defensive midfield player. I think he is a brilliant midfield player, he is box-to-box, but I think in a big game, in a one-off game, to go and win the Premier League or the Champions League, I think you need a specialist. Liverpool showed that with Fabinho. I still think they will address this position, but credit Gravenberch."

HEAD COACH: ARNE SLOT
"All the players have so much experience that they understand six games into the season doesn't give you a realistic view. That is more like in 19 games then you can really feel, 'Okay, where are we?' But it helps if you get good results, especially if you bring in a new manager and a new staff and being a successor of such a successful one."

FOR THE RECORD:
Ibrahima Konate's goal was his first in the Premier League and made him the first Liverpool player to score his first five goals with headers since Mark Wright in 1993.

ALSO THIS WEEKEND:
Manchester United 0-3 Tottenham Hotspur
Newcastle United 1-1 Manchester City
Arsenal 4-2 Leicester City

Alisson into an early save, Trent Alexander-Arnold was booked for fouling Jorgen Strand Larsen and the Norwegian also headed a cross over. Matheus Cunha tried to beat Alisson with a curler, but he dived to his right to clutch his fellow Brazilian's shot with Strand Larsen ready to pounce on a fumble.

In the opening half-an-hour the Reds created little, but with their new, patient approach under Slot, and having won 14 of their last 15 Premier League games against Wolverhampton Wanderers, nobody was pressing the panic button.

When Andre was booked for a lunging challenge on Mac Allister just outside the Wolves box it gave Alexander-Arnold an opportunity to shoot. Salah rolled the ball to him, but Sam Johnstone handled his low shot well. However, from that moment on Liverpool bossed the game and should have taken the lead through Dominik Szoboszlai.

Virgil van Dijk cut the Wolves defence open with a pass to Andy Robertson and Szoboszlai arrived to meet the Scot's low first-time cross just five yards out, but volleyed the ball against the back of Johnstone's left calf and it deflected wide.

Szoboszlai couldn't believe he hadn't scored, but it was a short stay of execution for Gary O'Neil's side. When a corner was cleared, Gravenberch recycled the ball to Jota on the left and after darting past Strand Larsen he crossed for Ibrahima Konate to rise highest and score with a downward header that Johnstone couldn't keep out.

It should have been 2-0 early in the second half. Johnstone, on the edge of his box, passed the ball to Mario Lemina, who tried to spread it wide but directed it straight to Salah. He struck the bouncing ball immediately with his right foot, but directed it wide of an open goal – a real collector's item.

Salah was ruing the miss even more four minutes later when Rayan Ait-Nouri equalised. Konate tried to let a ball run through to Alisson, but misjudged it and Strand Larsen got there first. Carlos Forbs mis-kicked the Norwegian's pull-back, but the ball ran to Ait-Nouri, who netted from close range.

A response was required and it came three minutes later when Alexander-Arnold crossed for Jota, who was hauled to the ground by his neck by Nelson Semedo. He protested, but it would have been a penalty had he been playing rugby league for Warrington Wolves.

Salah stepped up and shot one way, Johnstone dived the other way and Liverpool led 2-1, a scoreline that wouldn't change.

Johnstone palmed another Salah effort out, Konate made a vital block from Forbs and Curtis Jones, on as a sub, forced the Wolves keeper into a smart save from another move that Gravenberch orchestrated.

It denied the player-of-the-match the assist his performance deserved, but not Liverpool the points.

CRYSTAL PALACE FC 0
LIVERPOOL FC 1

Goal: Jota (9)
05.10.24 · Selhurst Park
Attendance: 25,185
Referee: Simon Hooper

PRESS BOX:
BARNEY RONAY, THE GUARDIAN
"Liverpool occupied Selhurst Park like a team of peacekeepers. This was a team in eco mode, regenerative braking football, a game of mature and sensible throttle management. Palace will be criticised for lacking aggression in the first half. But Liverpool also bring this on. They're basically chloroforming you in those moments. Give in to it. Sleep."

PUNDIT:
JOE COLE, TNT SPORTS
"Liverpool have been sensational. Alexander-Arnold and Salah on the right and Curtis Jones. When the defenders come out they're running into those spaces, it's where the goal came from. They've been fantastic at breaking it down."

CRYSTAL PALACE (3-4-3): Henderson, Lacroix, Guehi (C), Chalobah (Kamada 88), Munoz (Clyne 17), Wharton (Hughes 60), Lerma, Mitchell (Mateta 60), Sarr, Nketiah, Eze. Subs not used: Turner, Ward, Schlupp, Umeh, Kporha. Booked: Lerma, Hughes, Sarr, Nketiah.

LIVERPOOL (4-2-3-1): Alisson (Jaros 79), Alexander-Arnold, Konate, Van Dijk (C), Robertson (Tsimikas 79), Gravenberch, Mac Allister (Szoboszlai 46), Salah (Diaz 73), Jones (Endo 89), Gakpo, Jota. Subs not used: Gomez, Nunez, Quansah, Bradley. Booked: Gakpo, Mac Allister.

CRYSTAL PALACE FC v LIVERPOOL FC

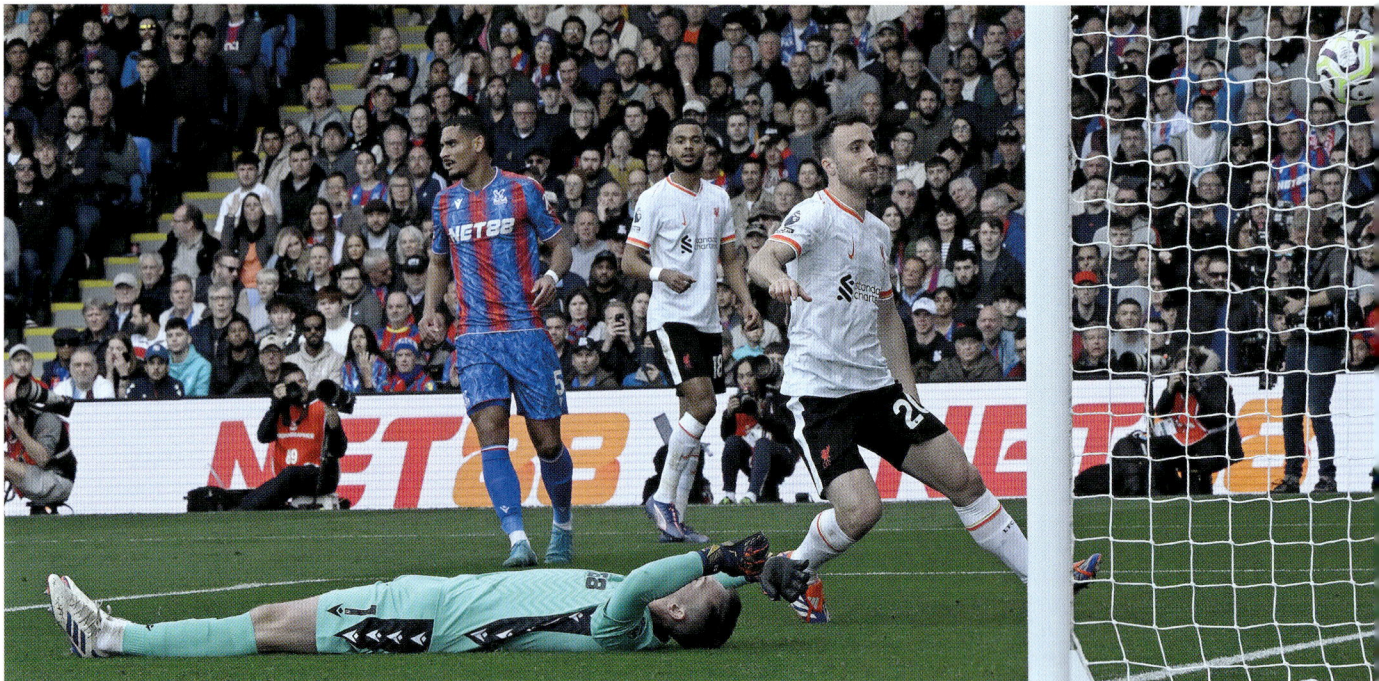

HEAD COACH: ARNE SLOT

"I think you saw how much we controlled the first 60 minutes. Then we had for 15 to 20 minutes a difficult spell. And then in the last 10 minutes we took control again. We took control by having a very good build-up and that helps to also tire the opponents because they have to defend a lot, they have to run a lot to make it difficult for us. And then the work-rate our attackers and midfielders put in is also extraordinary."

FOR THE RECORD:

Vitezslav Jaros became the fourth goalkeeper to make his Liverpool debut as a substitute after Mike Hooper (1986), Patrice Luzi (2004) and Adrian (2019).

ALSO THIS WEEKEND:

Brighton & Hove Albion 3-2 Tottenham Hotspur
Manchester City 3-2 Fulham
Brentford 5-3 Wolverhampton Wanderers

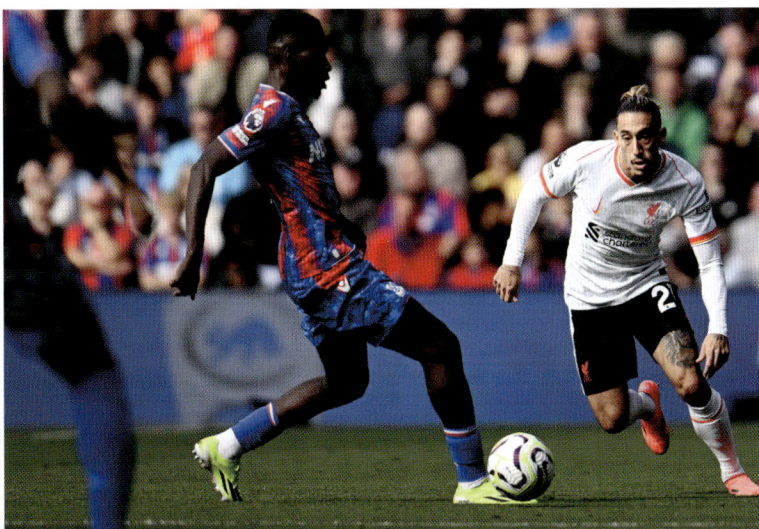

REPORT:

'Crystanbul', they called it, when a Liverpool team chasing the Premier League title blew a 3-0 lead at Selhurst Park to leave Manchester City in pole position.

That was a decade ago in 2013/14, when a Brendan Rodgers side featuring Luis Suarez, Daniel Sturridge, Raheem Sterling, Philippe Coutinho and Steven Gerrard played exhilarating football, but conceded 50 goals. Arne Slot's Liverpool are made of stronger stuff.

The class of 2024/25 still have plenty of exciting attacking talent, but are more pragmatic than the Reds of the Rodgers and Jürgen Klopp eras. While perhaps not as defensively-minded as Gerard Houllier and Rafa Benitez, who at times would both play central defenders at full-back with full-backs in midfield, Slot has instilled a new sense of control, of calmness, of composure during his first three months.

It was certainly in evidence during this 1-0 win when even the loss of Alisson, on an afternoon when Caoimhin Kelleher was unavailable due to illness, didn't lead to the kind of defensive collapse that can undermine a title challenge.

Yes, there were only 11 minutes to go when Alisson suffered a hamstring injury and Czechia international goalie Vitezslav Jaros had to come on for a surprise debut, but back in 2014 the Eagles scored three goals in the final 11 minutes of that infamous 3-3. So the fact that Jaros came on in the 79th minute – the same minute when a Dwight Gayle goal had sparked Crystal Palace's comeback a decade ago – was somewhat symbolic.

Bar a second-half spell of around 15 minutes, which came after the already-booked Alexis Mac Allister was substituted at half-time, the Reds had Palace on strings, although only after an early scare at a sun-kissed Selhurst Park.

The Eagles kicked off, lumped the ball forward and with 21 seconds on the clock Ismaila Sarr crossed for Eddie Nketiah to clip the ball over Alisson. All eyes turned to the assistant referee in front of the travelling Kop in the Arthur Wait Stand, and up went his flag. VAR concurred and Oliver Glasner's side remained goalless.

Wearing their white-black-white third kit, a much-loved strip by traditionalists who recall those being Liverpool's change colours from 1931 to 1982, Slot's men opened the scoring with a move that was befitting of any era.

Kostas Tsimikas intercepted the ball and so began a move that involved 10 passes between seven different players before an eighth finished it off. Tsimikas to Mac Allister to Curtis Jones to Ibrahima Konate to Virgil van Dijk to Tsimikas to Ryan Gravenberch to Van Dijk to Tsimikas to Cody Gakpo to Diogo Jota to the net. Poetry in motion, tra la la, la la.

It was the ninth pass, an incisive forward ball by Tsimikas to set Gakpo racing in behind right wing-back Daniel Munoz, that did the damage. Palace's right-sided defender Maxence Lacroix had to come across to cover, but got nowhere near Gakpo before he fired in a cross that Jota met at pace to strike the ball past Dean Henderson.

Trent Alexander-Arnold forced Henderson into a dive to repel his powerful 29th-minute drive and Jota had a great chance to get a second from Gravenberch's cross, but screwed his side-footed effort across goal.

Alisson was called into action to keep out a Sarr shot and after the break Mo Salah brilliantly brought down Van Dijk's pass in the box, but Henderson saved with his foot. When Jota timed his run perfectly to meet Alexander-Arnold's free-kick a goal seemed inevitable, but he glanced his header wide when he really had to score.

Palace got a foothold in the game and Alisson was forced to save a Nketiah shot and a powerful effort from Eberechi Eze, so when the Liverpool 'keeper injured a hamstring while clearing the ball long it was a concerning development.

He limped off and on came 23-year-old Jaros for his debut, but with Van Dijk and Konate protecting him, and Wataru Endo also introduced, the Czech had just one save to make, from Eze on a counter-attack, as Liverpool saw out the game without anything like a mini 'Crystanbul' looking likely.

LIVERPOOL FC 2
CHELSEA FC 1

Goals: Salah (29pen), Jackson (48), Jones (51)
20.10.24 · Anfield · Attendance: 60,277
Referee: John Brooks

LIVERPOOL (4-2-3-1): Kelleher, Alexander-Arnold (Gomez 81), Konate, Van Dijk (C), Robertson, Gravenberch, Jones (Mac Allister 81), Salah, Szoboszlai, Gakpo (Diaz 66), Jota (Nunez 30). Subs not used: Jaros, Endo, Tsimikas, Quansah, Morton. Booked: Slot, Nunez, Konate, Mac Allister.

CHELSEA (4-2-3-1): Sanchez, James (C) (Veiga 53), Adarabioyo (Badiashile 53), Colwill, Gusto, Caicedo, Lavia (Fernandez 53), Sancho (Neto 46), Palmer, Madueke (Nkunku 76), Jackson. Subs not used: Bettinelli, Disasi, Felix, Dewsbury-Hall. Booked: Adarabioyo, Jackson, Viega.

PRESS BOX:
IAN HERBERT, DAILY MAIL
"It had been a tense, febrile, absorbing occasion, which raged until the very last, was in the balance until the very last, and ultimately needed the collective will of the Anfield crowd to see Liverpool home. But the level of elation from Slot's players at the end told the story of a side who needed a win of real significance."

PUNDIT:
RAFA BENITEZ, BBC MATCH OF THE DAY 2
"I'm always looking for a midfielder that understands what is going on around him. Curtis Jones is watching behind, he can see the space. When Liverpool is three on three under pressure, he goes to the wide areas away from the two holding midfielders. He finds the space and goes forward. If he cannot, he goes backwards and keeps the ball. For his goal, you see a change of pace and the timing to get into the box. After, he finishes with the right foot, which is quite difficult."

REPORT:
Chelsea must have wished Curtis Jones had taken paternity leave.

The Liverpool midfielder's partner, Saffie, had given birth to baby Giselle seven days before this intense Anfield encounter, making Jones a father for the first time, but he swapped changing nappies to making Kopites happy with an all-action display.

Having missed both of the Reds' Carabao Cup final wins against Chelsea, and been an unused substitute against them in the 2022 FA Cup final success, Curtis was due a big day against the west Londoners.

It came in the form of a winning goal, being awarded two penalties and making a goal-saving block. Yet Jones wasn't the only central figure in the 75th clash between these two rivals this century, which was preceded by a period of applause for the late Peter Cormack.

Arne Slot politely described some of referee John Brooks' decisions as 'eventful', The Guardian newspaper called them 'perplexing'. The first controversy involving the officials came after just seven minutes.

Mo Salah played a long ball forward and Diogo Jota would have been clean though had he not been dragged to the ground by Tosin Adarabioyo. Just 24 hours earlier Arsenal's William Saliba had been red carded at Bournemouth for an almost identical foul, but Brooks decided a yellow card was sufficient with VAR official Michael Oliver backing him up.

To say Anfield was up in arms was an understatement, especially as Jota had to go off later in the half due to a rib injury suffered when Adarabioyo landed on him.

Chelsea keeper Robert Sanchez got lucky when his attempted pass

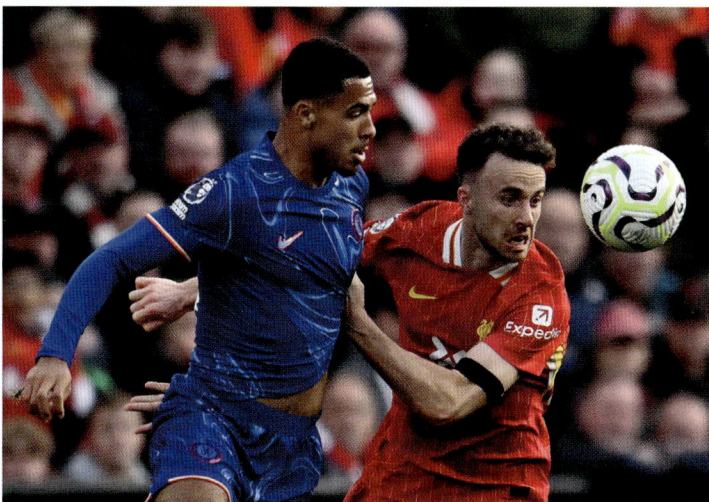

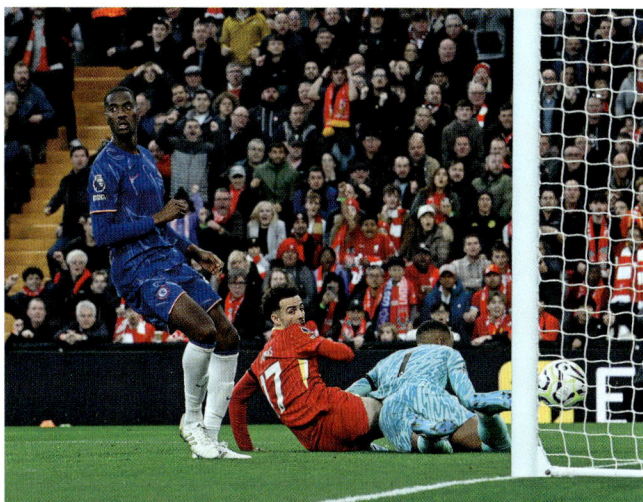

HEAD COACH: ARNE SLOT

"It was an equal game, in my opinion. There were phases in the game where we had to work really hard not to concede, but it's very pleasing to see that is also what we did. I think we all saw the great block tackles Dominik and Curtis had – Curtis first half, Dominik second half. Those moments are just as crucial as the goals we scored and added to that, there were a lot of eventful decisions by the referee, which made it the game it was."

FOR THE RECORD:

This was Liverpool's 50th Anfield win against Chelsea and, including penalty shoot-outs, the club's 3,000th victory overall in all competitions.

ALSO THIS WEEKEND:

Bournemouth 2-0 Arsenal
Wolverhampton Wanderers 1-2 Manchester City
Newcastle United 0-1 Brighton & Hove Albion

was blocked by Cody Gakpo and ricocheted into his arms rather than the goal, but the visitors had gradually dug a foothold in the game.

They almost took a 26th-minute lead, when Noni Madueke shrugged off Andy Robertson and laid the ball on a platter for Cole Palmer, but as he tried to shoot Jones slid in to make a crucial tackle followed by a block. From Robertson's clearance, Salah escaped some physical attention from Levi Colwill before breaking into the box and going down under a challenge from the Chelsea defender. The ref wagged his finger and played on, but moments later he was pointing to the spot.

Salah's shot was blocked by Colwill, but as he tried to prevent the loose ball running to Jones he tripped Liverpool's no17. Salah smashed the penalty past Sanchez for his fifth goal against his former club.

Liverpool were in the ascendancy. Jones won a header in midfield and slipped a pass to Salah, who crossed for Gakpo to convert at the far post, but the offside flag was up.

Chelsea remained a threat. Jackson clipped the outside of Caoimhin Kelleher's post, but in first-half stoppage-time Jones was awarded another penalty.

Darwin Nunez, on for Jota, played a pass for Jones to run onto and as Sanchez came out to meet him he upended the midfielder. However, this time Brooks was sent to the pitchside screen for a second look and decided the Chelsea goalie had made contact with the ball first before sending Jones head over heels. The penalty was overturned, Sanchez's yellow card cancelled and Slot booked instead for protesting.

Palmer curled an effort narrowly over as a lively first period concluded and Chelsea had the ball in the net three minutes after the restart when Caicedo again played Jackson in.

Up went the offside flag, but Ibrahima Konate's foot was playing the Senegalese striker on and VAR intervened. Chelsea were level, but not for long.

Dominik Szoboszlai played the ball out to Salah on the right and he clipped a lovely cross into the box. Enzo Maresca's men held their line on the edge of the penalty area, but nobody tracked the run of Jones from a deeper position and after controlling the ball with his left foot, he poked it past Sanchez with his right.

It was a winning goal from a new dad that will have given Chelsea sleepless nights and sent Kopites to bed dreaming of where seven wins from eight could lead.

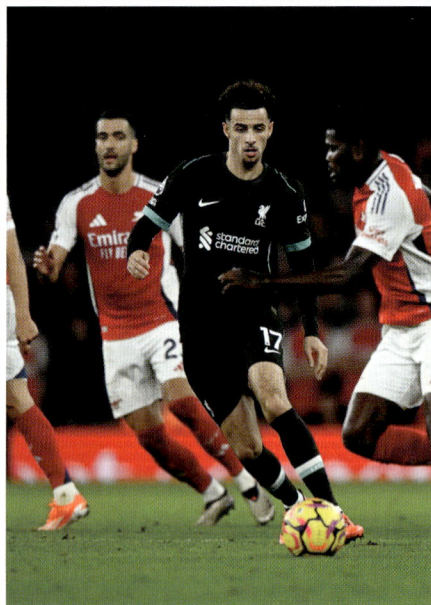

ARSENAL FC v LIVERPOOL FC

REPORT:

Arne Slot may have only been Liverpool manager for four months, but he gets it.

The Reds headed to the Emirates top of the Premier League, but amidst talk from those who will do anything to avoid giving Liverpool praise that Slot's side were only leaders because they 'hadn't played anyone'.

So after his side came back to draw 2-2 against Arsenal he addressed the issue in a post-match interview with Sky Sports.

"What surprises me is that people are saying we had an easy start, because everyone that has worked in the Premier League, or is still working here, was telling me before I came here that there are no easy games in the Premier League. Now all of a sudden there are many easy games."

The Liverpool head coach cited the win at Manchester United, the home victory against Chelsea and this hard-fought draw at Arsenal as evidence that his side hadn't risen to the top by playing the Dog & Duck every week.

Nottingham Forest deserve a mention too, yet despite Slot

becoming the first manager in English top-flight history to record 11 wins from his first 12 games in charge in all competitions when the Reds beat RB Leipzig 1-0 in the UEFA Champions League in midweek, drawing at Arsenal allowed Manchester City to go top and the doubters to continue doubting.

With Alisson and Diogo Jota still missing, and William Saliba and Riccardo Calafiori absent for the Gunners, both teams made tactical changes with Curtis Jones coming in to effectively have Liverpool lining up in a 4-2-4 system, while Mikel Arteta switched Ben White centrally, Jurrien Timber to left-back and Thomas Partey to right-back.

An early off-the-ball tussle between Virgil van Dijk and Kai Havertz indicated both sides were ready to battle and it was first blood to Arsenal in the ninth minute when Bukayo Saka ran onto a long ball, got past Andy Robertson and smashed a rising shot past Caoimhin Kelleher at his near post.

Arsenal almost gifted the Reds an equaliser four minutes later when Mikel Merino allowed a Saka pass to squirm under his foot and, with

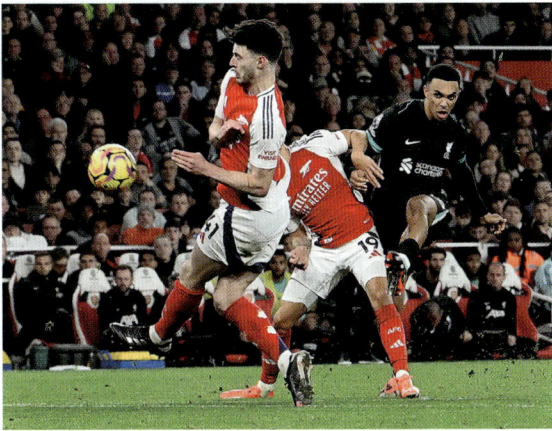

ARSENAL FC 2
LIVERPOOL FC 2

Goals: Saka (9), Van Dijk (18), Merino (43), Salah (81)

27.10.24 · Emirates Stadium
Attendance: 60,383
Referee: Anthony Taylor

ARSENAL (4-4-2): Raya, Partey, White, Gabriel (Kiwior 54), Timber (Lewis-Skelly 76), Saka (C) (Jesus 85), Rice, Merino, Martinelli (Nwaneri 85), Havertz, Trossard. Subs not used: Neto, Zinchenko, Jorginho, Sterling, Nichols. Booked: Raya, Jesus.

LIVERPOOL (4-2-4): Kelleher, Alexander-Arnold, Konate, Van Dijk (C), Robertson (Tsimikas 63), Gravenberch, Mac Allister (Szoboszlai 63), Salah, Jones (Endo 90+1), Nunez, Diaz (Gakpo 63). Subs not used: Jaros, Davies, Gomez, Quansah, Morton. Booked: Mac Allister, Hulshoff, Slot, Nunez.

PRESS BOX:
JAMES GHEERBRANT, THE TIMES
"Liverpool were not at their best, and Slot's tactics initially exerted little grip. But the team showed resilience, and the manager a decisive ruthless streak. A bold triple change early in the second half rescued a drifting performance, with the athleticism and range of Dominik Szoboszlai and the thrust of Kostas Tsimikas in particular giving Liverpool more purchase in the match."

PUNDIT:
MARTIN KELLY, LFCTV
"It was by far Liverpool's biggest test so far this season. I thought the subs that came on made a real impact. Tsimikas is going from strength to strength and especially in possession I thought he was a massive threat going forward along the left with Gakpo."

HEAD COACH: ARNE SLOT
"Going two times behind against a very strong and good Arsenal team and then to get a point is pleasing to see, especially because we had to play an away game in Europe this week. We had one day less to recover and to prepare and then to go two times behind and us coming back so strongly [in the] second half is very pleasing."

FOR THE RECORD:
This was the 22nd game Virgil van Dijk has scored in for Liverpool and the first time the Reds haven't won when he has netted.

ALSO THIS WEEKEND:
Chelsea 2-1 Newcastle United
West Ham United 2-1 Manchester United
Crystal Palace 1-0 Tottenham Hotspur

David Raya off his line, Mo Salah bent a first-time effort goalwards from 25 yards, but it glided past the post.

It was the first sign the pendulum was swinging in Liverpool's favour and when the clock struck 18, the Redmen were level. Luis Diaz forced a corner, Trent Alexander-Arnold whipped it in to the near post where the Colombian flicked on for Van Dijk to nod home from inside the six-yard box.

Saka curled a shot wide and Havertz blazed a half-volley over as the home fans howled for a penalty after Ibrahima Konate challenged Gabriel Martinelli, but replays showed he got the ball.

The Gunners are a danger from set-pieces and a free-kick, awarded for a Diaz foul on Partey, led to them going back ahead two minutes before the interval. Declan Rice curled the ball in and Merino got in behind Konate to head home, although a lengthy VAR check for offside was needed before it was given.

Alexis Mac Allister forced Raya to save his header from Alexander-Arnold's cross and Diaz came even closer to levelling when he dribbled around Partey and squeezed a shot past Raya, only to strike the post.

Losing Gabriel to injury was a blow to the hosts and after Slot introduced Kostas Tsimikas, Dominik Szoboszlai and Cody Gakpo in a 63rd-minute treble substitution it was all Liverpool.

Gravenberch blasted over and when Raya got booked for time wasting with 24 minutes still to play it showed just how nervous Arsenal were getting. There was also an unfortunate yellow card for Slot when fourth official Sam Barrott mistakenly thought something he shouted at Konate was directed towards him.

Martinelli tried to run the clock down by keeping possession near the corner flag from as early as the 76th minute, psychologically signalling that only one team was trying to score and five minutes later they did.

Alexander-Arnold clipped a pass down the line, Darwin Nunez ran onto it and played a lovely square ball between two retreating defenders for Salah to open the club face of his left boot and guide the ball home.

It felt like a big goal and meant the Reds not only had a first draw of the season to make it 22 points from a possible 27, but nobody could now say they hadn't played anyone.

LIVERPOOL FC 2
BRIGHTON & HOVE ALBION FC 1

Goals: Kadioglu (14), Gakpo (70), Salah (72)

02.11.24 · Anfield · Attendance: 60,331

Referee: Tony Harrington

PRESS BOX:

LEWIS STEELE, DAILY MAIL

"Arne Slot has done a remarkable job in stamping his authority on his new employers given he has been operating in the shadow of his legendary predecessor. But this victory had all the hallmarks of a Jürgen Klopp classic. The Mentality Monsters were back, to use the old phrase Klopp coined, as the Reds showed resilience in abundance as they fought back from a goal down."

PUNDIT:

JAMIE CARRAGHER, SKY SPORTS

"There's something about it, the Anfield factor. We know it happens, I felt it as a player. I played for two defensive managers, Gerard Houllier and Rafa Benitez. It doesn't matter what style you have, what system you want to play, at times, when you're a manager of Liverpool Football Club, Anfield just takes you on a ride, sweeps your feet away, and basically you cannot control that as a manager."

LIVERPOOL (4-2-3-1): Alisson, Alexander-Arnold, Konate (Gomez 46), Van Dijk (C), Tsimikas, Gravenberch, Mac Allister (Jones 66), Salah (Bradley 90+1), Szoboszlai (Diaz 66), Gakpo, Nunez (Endo 77). Subs not used: Jaros, Robertson, Quansah, Morton. Booked: Mac Allister.

BRIGHTON & HOVE ALBION (4-4-2): Verbruggen, Veltman (Gruda 76), Van Hecke, Igor Julio, Estupinan, Kadioglu (Moder 87), Hinshelwood (Ferguson 88), Ayari (Wieffer 76), Mitoma (Adringa 87), Rutter, Welbeck (C). Subs not used: Steele, Lamptey, Ensico, Baleba. Booked: Kadioglu.

REPORT:

On a day when Arsenal lost at Newcastle and Manchester City were beaten at Bournemouth, Liverpool showed character, resolve and determination to overturn a half-time deficit and beat Brighton & Hove Albion at Anfield.

It was the type of comeback victory that underpins a title challenge as not only did seeing off the Seagulls turn zero points into three, it meant the Reds had taken full advantage of their title rivals slipping up.

Had Brighton clung onto their lead the sense of frustration at a wasted opportunity would have been palpable inside Anfield, yet instead Liverpool supporters left the stadium bouncing after two goals in three second-half minutes put the Redmen top of the table.

At the age of 31, new Brighton boss Fabian Hürzeler is the youngest head coach in Premier League history. Born in Houston, Texas, in 1993,

he's 17 days younger than Wataru Endo, while Virgil van Dijk and Mo Salah were probably kicking a ball around by the time he was entering the world.

Having taken St Pauli from near relegation to German football's third tier to promotion to the Bundesliga in less than 18 months, the Seagulls swooped and on the evidence of the first half at Anfield it looks a shrewd call.

The sides had met in the Carabao Cup in midweek, Cody Gakpo's double decisive in a 3-2 Liverpool success at the AMEX Stadium, but the Dutchman was the only Red to also start this game, whereas centre-backs Igor Julio and Jean Paul van Hecke, plus right-sided midfielder Ferdi Kagioglu, remained in Hürzeler's side.

After a cagey opening nine minutes, somebody switched Darwin

HEAD COACH: ARNE SLOT

"I added after the game to the players that 45 minutes of the football we played in the first half will, in the end, punish you somewhere. So we need to show up from the start. The crowd was incredible the second half, our fans were incredible the second half. Our players were too, but our fans as well. It was the loudest crowd since I've been here."

FOR THE RECORD:

This was the first time Liverpool had beaten the same opponents twice in four days since defeating Manchester City twice in October 1995.

ALSO THIS WEEKEND:

Bournemouth 2-1 Manchester City
Newcastle United 1-0 Arsenal
Southampton 1-0 Everton

Nunez on and the Uruguayan created a solo chance through a mixture of skill and power.

Trent Alexander-Arnold's clearance deflected towards Nunez and, inside the centre-circle of his own half, he delicately flicked the ball over Joel Veltman before bulldozing his way past Kadioglu, who ended up on the deck. Nunez burst forward into the penalty area, cut back inside to go past Veltman again and curled a lovely shot goalwards only for Bart Verbruggen to fling himself to his left to fingertip the ball wide, preventing an outstanding individual goal.

Five minutes later, Brighton went ahead when Kaoru Mitoma's misplaced pass flicked off Danny Welbeck to Kadioglu, who struck a cross-shot from 12 yards that Caoimhin Kelleher got a glove on, but the ball flew in off the inside of the post.

One nil to the Albion and by half-time they could have had more. Georginio Rutter got in behind Van Dijk, but Kelleher won their one-v-one battle, and from a slick, flowing, counter-attack Mitoma crossed for the unmarked Kadioglu, but he blazed his volley into the Kop. Welbeck also curled a direct free-kick inches wide with Kelleher beaten. The half-time whistle was much needed for the Reds.

Arne Slot made a couple of tactical tweaks with Joe Gomez brought on for the injured Ibrahima Konate, but it was a change in attitude and intensity that ultimately swung this game in Liverpool's favour. The real Redmen turned up and almost got a 47th-minute leveller from the most unlikely of sources.

Kostas Tsimikas curled in a free-kick and the unmarked Gomez craned his neck to head goalwards, but directed the ball straight at Verbruggen. One day!

With the Anfield crowd lifted, the Reds perked up. Ex-Brighton midfielder Mac Allister forced Verbruggen to tip his diving header wide before Van Dijk, still up from a set-piece, only needed to connect with an arcing Alexander-Arnold pass to score, but missed the ball.

When Mo Salah left Pervis Estupinan trailing in his wake to run onto Nunez's flick you'd have put the mortgage on him to score, but he mishit his attempted dink over Verbruggen, who pawed the ball down.

Gakpo also curled a shot narrowly wide but it felt like the dam was about to burst and it soon did. Gakpo cut inside again and clipped in a cross that was intended for Nunez, but evaded everyone and bounced into the net with Verbruggen rooted to his line.

All of a sudden the Anfield whirlpool that has swallowed so many opponents over the years had Brighton by the ankles.

Before they knew it, Curtis Jones had driven forward, exchanged passes with fellow substitute Luis Diaz, and slipped a pass to Salah, who cut past Estupinan and smashed an unstoppable left-footed effort in at the Kop net.

Momentum had created bedlam and a significant win on a day when others had lost.

LIVERPOOL FC 2
ASTON VILLA FC 0

Goals: Nunez (20), Salah (84)
09.11.24 · Anfield · Attendance: 60,292
Referee: David Coote

LIVERPOOL (4-2-3-1): Kelleher, Alexander-Arnold (Bradley 25), Konate, Van Dijk (C), Robertson, Gravenberch, Mac Allister (Endo 87), Salah, Jones (Szoboszlai 65), Diaz, Nunez (Gakpo 65). Subs not used: Jaros, Gomez, Tsimikas, Quansah, Morton.

ASTON VILLA (4-2-3-1): Martinez (C), Konsa, Carlos, Torres, Digne (Maatsen 74), Onana (Kamara 74), Tielemans, Bailey (Philogene 65), Rogers, Ramsey (McGinn 45+2), Watkins (Duran 65). Subs not used: Olsen, Mings, Buendia, Bogarde. Booked: Rogers, Tielemans, Kamara.

PRESS BOX:
JONATHAN NORTHCROFT, THE SUNDAY TIMES
"Was Mohamed Salah's timeless brilliance better than Ibrahima Konate's immense resistance? Take your pick. Both were signatures of a victory acclaimed by a rowdy Saturday night crowd at Anfield."

PUNDIT:
MICAH RICHARDS, BBC MATCH OF THE DAY
"Austin MacPhee [Aston Villa's set-piece coach] has got them so well drilled, but Liverpool turned Villa's strength into their weakness. Villa committed men forward but it left an ocean of space. They didn't know how to deal with the pace of Salah and Nunez. From a defensive perspective someone has to get tight or drop off. They were sort of in between. Aston Villa just couldn't get it right and Liverpool capitalised on that."

HEAD COACH: ARNE SLOT

"We did put effort in defending them from scoring because that was also today their main threat, in my opinion, their set-pieces. So we had to do a lot to prevent them from scoring. And then these counter-breaks had nothing to do with what we do on the training ground or what we tell them before. That is pure quality and purely what the players come up with in these transition moments."

FOR THE RECORD:

Mo Salah got his 10th assist in his 17th appearance of the season, the quickest a Liverpool player has reached double figures since John Barnes created 10 goals in 18 games in 1987/88.

ALSO THIS WEEKEND:

Brighton & Hove Albion 2-1 Manchester City
Tottenham Hotspur 1-2 Ipswich Town
Chelsea 1-1 Arsenal

REPORT:

In a game of fine margins it was Aston Villa's biggest strength that also proved to be their biggest weakness thanks to Liverpool's ability to exploit their Achilles Heel.

Under Unai Emery the Villans have been transformed from mid-table also-rans to Champions League contenders. A big part of Villa's upward trajectory has been down to Austin MacPhee, the Scottish set-piece coach. Aston Villa finished fourth in 2023/24 having scored 25 goals from set-pieces, the most by any club in Europe's top five leagues.

So when Arne Slot and his coaching staff prepared the Reds for this Saturday night fixture, defending set-pieces was a prime focus.

It was necessary, as Villa caused the Redmen problems from dead balls, but what the visitors evidently hadn't accounted for was Liverpool's threat on the counter-attack from their corners. Their biggest asset proved to be their biggest vulnerability and was how this match was settled.

Xabi Alonso had returned to Anfield in midweek with Bayer Leverkusen in the Champions League, but was on the end of a 4-0 reverse. Luis Diaz, switched to a central role, scored the first hat-trick of his career, but he returned to his more familiar left-sided position with Darwin Nunez central.

Anfield fell silent before kick-off, bar the sound of a lone trumpet playing The Last Post, as those who had served their country were remembered ahead of Armistice Day. When the action got underway it was Ollie Watkins who curled the first attempt of note over with both sides also having a couple of efforts blocked.

Ibrahima Konate conceded a corner in the 19th minute, and as Youri Tielemans whipped the ball in, half of the players on the pitch were in Liverpool's six-yard box. But when Alexis Mac Allister cleared it was Virgil van Dijk who got to it first.

At the precise moment the Liverpool skipper glanced up he had three team-mates sprinting forward with only two Villa players covering, so clipped a first-time pass to set Mo Salah racing away with Leon Bailey trying to keep up.

The Villa winger tugged at Salah's shoulder, sent him crashing to the turf and landed on top of the Egyptian, but as Anfield howled at referee David Coote for a foul and red card, Nunez chased after the loose ball, which also tempted the initially backpedalling Villa goalkeeper Emi Martinez to head towards it. Nunez arrived first, shifted it to the left of the Argentine and from an increasingly acute angle beat the diving goalkeeper with a rising shot.

Liverpool lost Trent Alexander-Arnold to injury shortly afterwards, Conor Bradley coming on, and almost got a second goal from another Villa corner when Jacob Ramsey's shot was blocked by the Northern Ireland international and broke for Salah. Villa had all 10 outfield players within 20 yards of Caoimhin Kelleher's goal, allowing Salah to play Nunez clean through, but he shot into the Kop.

When Villa forced a corner off Andy Robertson in the 37th minute it was hard to know if it was advantageous for them or Liverpool, but this time Amadou Onana met Lucas Digne's curler with a header and Kelleher tipped the ball over. Another Digne corner came in and Kelleher produced an even better save from Diego Carlos before Ryan Gravenberch blocked Watkins' header from the rebound.

A minute into the second half, Morgan Rogers missed a golden chance to equalise when Konate landed awkwardly after heading clear and stayed down. It allowed the Villa midfielder time to shoot, but he bent the ball off target.

The decisive blow came in the 84th minute. Villa committed men forward for a throw-in deep in the Reds' half, but when Dominik Szoboszlai cleared, Diego Carlos headed the ball against Salah, who had more than half of the pitch to run into with nobody back.

Martinez opted to stay on his line, hoping the cavalry would arrive, but by the time they did Salah was six yards out and tucking the ball home before sitting on the advertising hoardings to celebrate a victory created on the counter-attack.

REPORT:

On paper, it looked like a done deal. Southampton, bottom of the table following one win from 11 games, versus Liverpool, top of the Premier League after nine wins in the same period. Away win.

But football isn't played on paper and with a howling wind whistling in off the south coast what may have looked like being a comfortable afternoon for Arne Slot's Reds was far from it.

The blustery conditions played their part with players misjudging the flight of the ball and making uncharacteristic errors, but ultimately Liverpool got the job done.

Russell Martin's Saints were promoted from the Championship via the play-offs by playing high-risk football, working the ball out from the back. They have stuck to their principles in the Premier League, but against top-level opposition errors get punished more clinically and the Saints went into this game having conceded a league-high six goals directly from mistakes. It was a trend that continued.

Manchester City's 4-0 home defeat to Spurs the previous day meant a Liverpool win would open up an eight-point gap at the top and the manner in which Dominik Szoboszlai burst through midfield

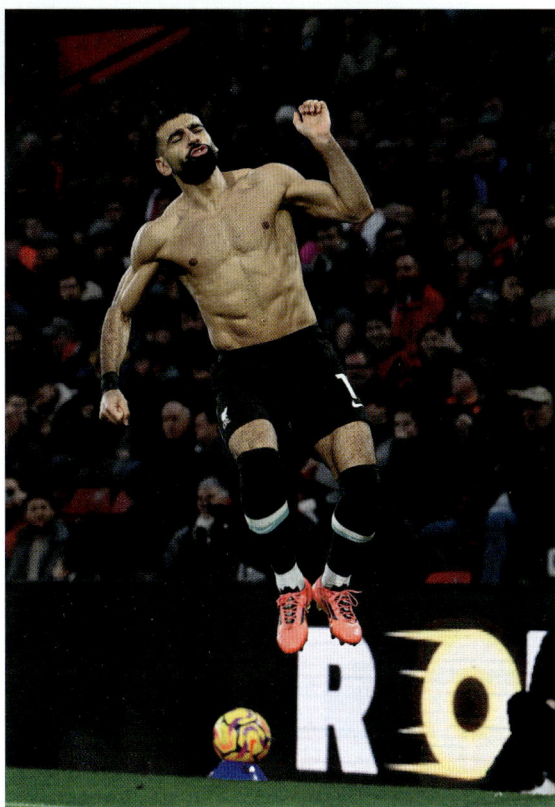

SOUTHAMPTON FC 2
LIVERPOOL FC 3

Goals: Szoboszlai (30), Armstrong (42), Fernandes (56), Salah (65, 83pen)

24.11.24 · St Mary's · Attendance: 31,278

Referee: Sam Barrott

SOUTHAMPTON (5-4-1): McCarthy, Walker-Peters, Harwood-Bellis, Downes, Stephens (C), Fraser (Sugawara 77), Dibling, Fernandes, Lallana (Aribo 37), Armstrong (Archer 77), Onuachu (Ugochukwu 62). Subs not used: Lumley, Manning, Bree, Brereton-Diaz, Sulemana. Booked: Lallana, Armstrong, Stephens.

LIVERPOOL (4-2-3-1): Kelleher, Bradley, Konate, Van Dijk (C), Robertson, Gravenberch, Jones (Mac Allister 62), Salah, Szoboszlai, Gakpo (Diaz 62), Nunez (Endo 90). Subs not used: Jaros, Davies, Gomez, Quansah, Morton, Elliott. Booked: Bradley, Konate, Gakpo, Salah.

PRESS BOX:
MIKE WALTERS, DAILY MIRROR
"Eight points clear – go on, count them. Mo Salah and Liverpool are going to take some stopping now. Only two sides – Newcastle in 1995 and Arsenal two years ago – have won 10 of their first 12 games and not gone on to win the Premier League title."

PUNDIT:
GLENN MURRAY, BBC RADIO FIVE LIVE
"It was a wonderful second half. It was open, it was honest. Liverpool going eight points clear is huge. Everyone has played the same amount of games too, no one has any games in hand, it is flat out after 12 games, Liverpool eight points clear. I don't think when Arne Slot took the job he could have imagined being so far ahead so early on."

HEAD COACH: ARNE SLOT
"In the second half I saw the intensity I was looking for in the first half. There was not enough urgency to arrive in the box, we just kept the ball instead of attacking the box. Although we fell behind in the second half we showed more urgency and intensity. That led to chances and eventually two goals."

FOR THE RECORD:
Mo Salah's second goal was his 100th away from Anfield in all competitions – only Roger Hunt and Ian Rush have previously reached an away century for Liverpool.

ALSO THIS WEEKEND:
Manchester City 0-4 Tottenham Hotspur
Arsenal 3-0 Nottingham Forest
Ipswich Town 1-1 Manchester United

in the sixth minute signalled intent. He slipped the ball to Mo Salah, but Alex McCarthy pushed the shot wide.

Conor Bradley got an early booking for hauling down ex-Red Adam Lallana, who was also booked for a rash, studs-up challenge on Ryan Gravenberch that deserved an 'orange card', if such a thing existed.

Ibrahima Konate was also cautioned for a foul and moments later Cody Gakpo picked open Southampton's five-man defensive line with a cross that floated over Ryan Fraser to Salah at the far post, but his half-volley was saved by McCarthy.

Szoboszlai was growing increasingly influential and after tackling Mateus Fernandes on the edge of the box had a snapshot saved by McCarthy.

Liverpool were camped outside the Southampton penalty area and when McCarthy gathered a weak Bradley shot it looked like another chance had gone, but the goalkeeper immediately rolled the ball to Fernandes on the 18-yard line.

Jones was alive to it and hunted the Portuguese down. The ball ran loose and Flynn Downes tried to prevent a corner, but only succeeded in playing it straight to Szoboszlai on the edge of the area. The Hungary skipper calmly took a touch before bending a left-footed shot in off the inside of the post.

In the 40th minute, the hosts had a lifeline when Virgil van Dijk was dispossessed bringing the ball forward and the covering Andy

Robertson tripped Tyler Dibling on the edge of the box. Referee Sam Barrott pointed to the spot, VAR agreed it was inside and although Caoimhin Kelleher produced a fine save from Adam Armstrong's penalty, the rebound fell to the Saints striker and he netted at the second attempt.

If that was a shock to the system then Arne Slot must have felt like he'd been zapped by a cattle-prod in the 56th minute when McCarthy spilling Robertson's corner inadvertently led to a counter-attack that ended with Fernandes scoring.

Slot responded by bringing on Alexis Mac Allister and Luis Diaz. Three minutes later it was 2-2. Darwin Nunez had narrowly failed to tee up Diaz after racing onto a Salah pass, but when Gravenberch chipped another ball forward McCarthy raced out of his goal only for Salah to nip in and touch the ball past him and into the net.

McCarthy redeemed himself by tipping over a Diaz header, but Liverpool continued to press. Salah glided another cross towards Robertson at the back post, but Yukinari Sugawara, who'd only just come on, misjudged it on the wind and as he leapt to chest the ball back to his goalkeeper used his hand instead for a penalty.

Salah smashed the spot-kick home and whipped off his shirt to celebrate with an ecstatic travelling Kop. Only the inside of the post prevented him completing his hat-trick, but he'd have taken three points over three goals anyway.

LIVERPOOL FC 2
MANCHESTER CITY FC 0

Goals: Gakpo (12), Salah (78pen)
01.12.24 · Anfield · Attendance: 60,248
Referee: Chris Kavanagh

LIVERPOOL (4-2-3-1): Kelleher, Alexander-Arnold (Quansah 73), Gomez, Van Dijk (C), Robertson, Gravenberch, Mac Allister, Salah (Jones 84), Szoboszlai, Diaz (Elliott 90+1), Gakpo (Nunez 73). Subs not used: Jaros, Davies, Endo, Morton, Nyoni.

MANCHESTER CITY (4-2-3-1): Ortega, Walker (C), Dias, Akanji, Ake, Silva, Gundogan (Savinho 58), Lewis (Grealish 79), Foden (De Bruyne 79), Nunes (Doku 57), Haaland. Subs not used: Ederson, Carson, Gvardiol, O'Reilly, McAtee. Booked: Nunes, Foden, Akanji.

PRESS BOX:
PAUL JOYCE, THE TIMES
"The gap, at times, resembled a gulf. Liverpool were superior in all departments; the athletic midfield of Ryan Gravenberch, Alexis Mac Allister and Dominik Szoboszlai ran roughshod over their opponents, the attack, with Salah scoring and assisting for the 36th occasion to match Wayne Rooney's record in the Premier League, was threatening where Erling Haaland was anonymous and the defence barely put a foot out of place. While City looked frazzled, Liverpool dazzled."

PUNDIT:
ROY KEANE, SKY SPORTS
"We have to praise the manager Arne Slot as he's doing a magnificent job, but the squad he took over were a decent group. He's added his personality to it. If you'd have been told that Liverpool would be in the position they are now, you wouldn't believe it. Their performances, their defence, their big players are turning up for the big occasion. It never felt like Liverpool were losing today. It's a combination of decision-making and quality."

HEAD COACH:
ARNE SLOT
"I've experienced already a few nice moments here as a manager but I think today stood out when it comes to the energy we delivered on the pitch, but also the energy the fans delivered for us. But if you want to win anything, it's all about consistency so let's not get carried away by one or two wins. It's all about consistency until the end of the season, keeping the players fit, keeping them playing with this much energy And like you probably saw today, I only had five defenders available. So to win something in the end, there's such a long way to go and so many challenges to take. But it's good that we are capable of winning against these teams in our own style."

FOR THE RECORD:
Mo Salah's goal was his eighth for Liverpool against the reigning champions – only Gordon Hodgson (nine) has scored more.

ALSO THIS WEEKEND:
West Ham United 2-5 Arsenal
Chelsea 3-0 Aston Villa
Manchester United 4-0 Everton

REPORT:
Four days after beating the Spanish and European champions, Liverpool saw off the English champions too.

Real Madrid had felt the full force of Anfield with Conor Bradley's ball-n-all challenge on Kylian Mbappe symbolic of a tubthumping 2-0 success, but this was Arne Slot's Reds at their relentless best.

From the first whistle they tore into Pep Guardiola's Manchester City like a pack of red-clad Tasmanian Devils in a field full of wallabies. The Cityzens simply had no answer. They were devoured. Taken apart. The 2-0 scoreline flattered them.

City arrived on the back of three consecutive Premier League defeats – five in all competitions – and with all the evidence suggesting losing Ballon d'Or winner Rodri to an ACL injury was the equivalent of taking the SIM card out of a smartphone.

When a rival is going through a tricky time, making the most of it is paramount if you've got serious designs on taking their crown and that's precisely what Liverpool did.

It may only have been the first day of December, but it felt like a changing of the guard.

Kyle Walker made the first mistake of the afternoon when he won the toss and made the Redmen kick towards the Kop. When that happens the Reds invariably start quicker, with greater intensity, and after just four minutes Ryan Gravenberch picked Ilkay Gundogan's pocket, Luis Diaz took it on and played Cody Gakpo through, who was denied by Stefan Ortega plunging to his right. The offside flag went up, but it was a signal of intent.

Ortega was called into action again four minutes later, this time to save from Dominik Szoboszlai after Gravenberch lapped up another stray pass. The overworked City 'keeper pushed another Szoboszlai effort out before the ball was scrambled out for a corner. Alexis Mac Allister and Szoboszlai worked it short and from the Hungarian's cross, Virgil van Dijk steamed in and powered a header across goal that thumped the inside of the post.

Anfield was bouncing, Liverpool were flying and City looked fuzzy-headed. A goal had to come and when it duly did in the 12th minute it was a work of art.

Trent Alexander-Arnold sprayed a glorious diagonal ball forward

from left to right, Salah chased it, brought the ball inside and dissected a static City defence, plus the diving Ortega, with an inch-perfect cross that Gakpo nudged home from two yards.

Alexander-Arnold almost played Salah in again with a pass from the edge of his own box so good it seemed unfair. Nathan Ake was forced to concede a corner that Mac Allister arrowed in and the unmarked Van Dijk met at pace, but headed narrowly wide.

City continued to play out from the back, but Alexander-Arnold pressed Matheus Nunes into an error, burst into the box to receive a Diaz pass and teed up Gakpo, but he skied his shot.

After 23 minutes the stats showed that Liverpool led 45-5 on touches in the opponents' final third and after having a breather for 10 minutes the Reds came close again. Salah forced a corner from a Joe Gomez pass and Alexander-Arnold grazed the base of the post after Mac Allister's dead ball was cleared to him.

Five minutes into the second period, Andy Robertson released Gakpo again, but Ortega spread himself to make a save. From the corner, Van Dijk again got there first, but glanced the ball over. On

another day the Liverpool skipper could've had a hat-trick.

Salah should also have netted when he robbed Manuel Akanji to sprint clear, but tried to bend the ball past Ortega and got too much loft on his club.

While the visitors were dominating second-half possession they failed to have a shot on target and it was Liverpool who continued to create. Salah shot wide, Gapko struck an effort straight at Ortega and Alexander-Arnold had a low drive blocked.

When Ruben Dias was caught on the ball by Darwin Nunez, Diaz nicked it past the challenge of Walker and tried to go around Ortega, but was sent sprawling to the turf. Penalty. Erling Haaland had a word with his 'keeper, but Salah slotted the ball low to Ortega's left before cupping his ear in celebration. Game. Over.

Caoimhin Kelleher finally had to make a save when a rare Van Dijk mistake allowed Kevin de Bruyne in, but the Kop were having too much fun teasing City boss Guardiola about his job prospects to be concerned.

They had witnessed a performance of champions elect.

NEWCASTLE UNITED FC v LIVERPOOL FC

NEWCASTLE UNITED FC 3
LIVERPOOL FC 3

Goals: Isak (35), Jones (50), Gordon (62), Salah (68, 83), Schar (90)

04.12.24 · St James' Park
Attendance: 52,237
Referee: Andy Madley

NEWCASTLE UNITED (4-3-3): Pope, Livramento, Schar, Burn, Hall, Tonali (Longstaff 87), Guimaraes (C), Joelinton (Willock 88), Murphy (Barnes 74), Isak, Gordon (Wilson 87). Subs not used: Dubravka, Targett, Kelly, Almiron, Osula. Booked: Tonali, Pope.

LIVERPOOL (4-2-3-1): Kelleher, Quansah, Gomez (Alexander-Arnold 67), Van Dijk (C), Robertson, Gravenberch (Szoboszlai 67), Mac Allister, Salah, Jones, Gakpo (Diaz 67), Nunez. Subs not used: Jaros, Nallo, Endo, Morton, Nyoni, Elliott. Booked: Mac Allister, Quansah, Gravenberch, Alexander-Arnold, Nunez.

PRESS BOX:
SAM WALLACE, DAILY TELEGRAPH
"This felt like another night of Salah triumph for a few pulsating moments and then the game swung again, borne along with the same volatile force that had gripped it from the start. It is 28 years since the great seven-goal Anfield shoot-out between these clubs, when English football was a much less strategic pursuit – a code that had not yet been broken by the weight of all the analysis and scrutiny. Yet the greatest compliment you could pay these teams was that they played in that spirit."

PUNDIT:
NEIL MELLOR, LFCTV
"It was a strange game because at half-time we were all saying take a point, but at 3-2 up so late in the game you're thinking we could have won this. It's the genius of Salah again and the three subs made a big difference. It was 2-1 at the time when they came on and I thought they gave us energy, but we ended up conceding so late. I know

Caoimhin Kelleher will be blamed for that goal because he made a mistake, but he made a massive save at 1-0 when Gordon went clean through. He makes a big, big save and I don't know if we'd have come back to get a point if we'd gone 2-0 down."

HEAD COACH: ARNE SLOT

"I think Mo had a massive impact on the game, but I think in general in the second half we played much, much better than the first half. In the first half we had a lot of problems with their intensity, aggressive playing style without the ball – aggressive in a good way. They forced us into too many mistakes. It wasn't that difficult for us to be better in the second half with the ball and that's what we were. Maybe it was difficult for them to keep the intensity of the first 45."

FOR THE RECORD:

Mo Salah scored in a seventh successive league match for the second time, having also done so in 2021. Only John Aldridge has achieved the same feat, in 1987 and 1989.

ALSO THIS MIDWEEK:

Manchester City 3-0 Nottingham Forest
Arsenal 2-0 Manchester United
Southampton 1-5 Chelsea

REPORT:

Had Liverpool won or lost this game nobody could have complained, so a 3-3 draw under the lights at St James' Park was probably a fair result. Yet the Reds left Tyneside tinged with disappointment because of how it happened.

Arne Slot's men overturned 1-0 and 2-1 deficits to lead 3-2 going into the last minute, but conceded an equaliser due to a rare error of judgment by Caoimhin Kelleher.

Such moments are part of the life of the goalkeeper, but without the Irishman's interventions in the previous 89 minutes the Reds wouldn't have been leading at that point anyway. It was Liverpool's first-half display Slot was more concerned about.

Right from the off, Newcastle showed more intent. They were intense and aggressive whereas Liverpool looked sluggish and gave the ball away frequently. It made for a corker of a game with the second half a throwback to the famous Anfield 4-3s of the 1990s, minus a winner.

Sandro Tonali forced Kelleher into an early save before Alexis Mac Allister struck a low half-volley that Nick Pope pushed wide. From Mac Allister's corner, the ball ended up back at the feet of the best there's been from the Argentine and he had a pop with his left, grazing the outside of the post. Four minutes later, Macca was harshly booked for blocking Fabian Schar to earn a one-game suspension that ruled him out of the weekend's Merseyside derby at Goodison Park until Storm Darragh intervened.

Newcastle's intensity was epitomised by boyhood Red Anthony Gordon in the 22nd minute when he battled to win possession off Mo Salah and began a move that ended with Jacob Murphy firing a cross-shot against Kelleher's post.

Joe Gomez also made a vital interception to prevent Lewis Hall getting in, but the Magpies were squawking and took the lead in the 35th minute. Bruno Guimaraes got past Mac Allister and fed Alexander Isak, who cut back outside Virgil van Dijk and unleashed an unstoppable shot from 20 yards into the top corner.

It could easily have been 2-0 three minutes later when Gomez miscued a backpass to leave Gordon one-on-one with Kelleher, but the Liverpool 'keeper blocked his shot and smothered the ball.

Murphy fired another effort wide and both Jarell Quansah, playing at right-back, and Ryan Gravenberch were booked before a much-needed half-time whistle. Not for the first time, whatever Slot said to his team in the dressing room psyched the Reds up and they were Ready to Rhumble.

Only five minutes had elapsed when Mac Allister picked off a stray pass, sent Salah scampering away down the right and he pulled the ball back with the outside of his boot for Curtis Jones to arrive at pace and clip home the equaliser.

All of a sudden the momentum had shifted. Cody Gakpo's half-volley was deflected narrowly wide by Schar and when Pope missed Salah's cross and Gakpo headed back across goal, Darwin Nunez was a boot size away from toeing the ball in. Then, against the run of play, Newcastle went ahead. Isak played a pass to Gordon, who cut inside Gomez and squeezed a shot past Kelleher.

St James' Park was bouncing and a game of basketball broke out. Jones met Andy Robertson's cross with a header from close range, but Pope pawed the ball away before Isak got in behind the Reds' defence and netted only for a belated offside flag to be raised.

Slot made a triple substitution and moments later it was 2-2 after two of the new arrivals, Trent Alexander-Arnold and Dominik Szoboszlai, worked the ball down the right. Alexander-Arnold pulled a low cross back and Salah guided the ball home with his right foot.

Anything could have happened after that and pretty much did. Murphy got to a through-ball before the advancing Kelleher, but shot wide. Luis Diaz had an effort blocked, but Nunez shanked the rebound past the post. Then Salah skinned Hall and struck a rising shot against the crossbar. The Egyptian King wasn't to be denied and with seven minutes to play he took an Alexander-Arnold pass on his right and spun onto his left before beating Pope to send the travelling Kop wild up in the gods.

It could, maybe should, have been the winner, but when Kelleher left alone a Guimaraes free-kick, thinking the ball was going out, Schar stole in at the far post to equalise on a night when both sides deserved to take something from a classic.

LIVERPOOL FC v FULHAM FC

REPORT:

You don't hear many ex-Everton managers praising the Anfield crowd, but Marco Silva was in no doubt that 10-man Liverpool still had an extra player after Andy Robertson was sent off.

"The game is emotional here," he said. "The crowd plays a big part and with the quality of Liverpool they can almost be unstoppable. I think the red card created more emotion in the game, the crowd played their part."

Silva was the Blues boss left stunned by Divock Origi's famous 96th-minute winner in the 2018/19 Anfield derby and was on the end of a 5-2 thrashing in 2019/20, but the atmosphere for Liverpool v Fulham games doesn't usually reach Merseyside derby fever pitch. This was different.

Liverpool were a goal down and a man down within 17 minutes, enough for fans of some clubs to write it off as a bad day at the office. Not at Anfield. Not when the Reds are leading a title race. And not with a burning sense of injustice in the air.

Only 61 seconds had been played when Issa Diop fouled Andy Robertson in the box with a knee-high challenge. An offside flag

LIVERPOOL FC 2
FULHAM FC 2

Goals: Pereira (11), Gakpo (47), Muniz (76), Jota (86)

14.12.24 · Anfield · Attendance: 60,333
Referee: Tony Harrington

LIVERPOOL (4-2-3-1): Alisson, Alexander-Arnold (Jota 79), Gomez, Van Dijk (C), Robertson, Jones (Quansah 70), Gravenberch, Salah, Szoboszlai (Elliott 79), Gakpo (Nunez 70), Diaz. Subs not used: Kelleher, Endo, Chiesa, Morton, Nyoni. Booked: Diaz, Jones, Slot, Nunez. Sent-off: Robertson (17).

FULHAM (4-2-3-1): Leno, Tete (Castagne 55), Diop, Cuenca, Robinson (C), Berge, Lukic, Wilson (Traore 87), Pereira (Smith-Rowe 79), Iwobi, Jimenez (Muniz 68). Subs not used: Benda, Vinicius, King, Sessegnon, Godo. Booked: Diop, Pereira, Robinson, Berge.

PRESS BOX:
PAUL GORST, LIVERPOOL ECHO
"The booing that echoed around Anfield at full time was not reserved for the efforts of the Liverpool players, who played around 90 minutes all in a man down. Nor were they aimed at Arne Slot, whose game-changing substitutes saved a point. Instead, they were directed squarely at the match officials and their colleagues on VAR, who Reds fans were clearly incensed by. The only question was which of the handful of decisions they felt most aggrieved by."

PUNDIT:
CHRIS SUTTON, BBC RADIO FIVE LIVE
"I thought Liverpool were phenomenal, it was a brilliant game. They went down to 10 men and didn't feel sorry for themselves. Jota looked sharp as anything. Fulham are a really balanced side and were a big threat down the left. Robinson looked great, but I thought Liverpool were phenomenal in the face of adversity."

HEAD COACH: ARNE SLOT
"I couldn't have asked for more. Dominated the game, more ball possession with 10 men, more chances created – everything what you want. Unfortunately for us, maybe the only chance they got with 10 men led to a goal – that sometimes happens as well."

FOR THE RECORD:
Andy Robertson was the first Liverpool player to ever be sent off against Fulham at Anfield and the first Red to be dismissed in December since getting sent off at Spurs in 2021.

ALSO THIS WEEKEND:
Arsenal 0-0 Everton
Manchester City 1-2 Manchester United
Southampton 0-5 Tottenham Hotspur

against Cody Gakpo meant the play was already dead, but referee Tony Harrington issued the Fulham defender a yellow card. Replays showed it could easily have been red, but VAR official Stuart Attwell said no.

To Anfield's incredulity, Luis Diaz was cautioned moments later for attempting to score with an overhead-kick and Andreas Pereira followed him into the book for leaving his studs in on Ryan Gravenberch's ankle, having made no attempt to play the ball. Again, it could've been red and Pereira rubbed salt into the wounds by scoring the opening goal.

Left-back Antonee Robinson burst forward on a Robertson-esque overlapping run and Pereira connected with his cross at the back post, the ball flicking off Robertson's thigh to go over Alisson.

There was worse to come for the Scot when he miscontrolled a Sasa Lukic crossfield pass and brought down former Reds winger Harry Wilson, who would have been through on goal, as he tried to atone for his error. Harrington brandished a straight red.

VAR checked for offside against Wilson and although the ball had rolled into a central area where Virgil van Dijk was covering, Robertson was sent for a 17th-minute shower. Wilson whistled the free-kick narrowly over.

Arne Slot had to readjust and switched to a bullish 3-4-2 system with Gravenberch joining Van Dijk and Joe Gomez in a back three, Trent Alexander-Arnold and Cody Gakpo operating as wide midfielders and Mo Salah moving centrally alongside Diaz.

Fulham dominated possession, but every shot they had seemed to be blocked by a Liverpool defender and it was Diaz who had the best chance, but he headed Dominik Szoboszlai's 41st-minute cross over from six yards out.

Early in the second half Gravenberch chased back to win a sliding challenge on Robinson near the corner flag and thus began a move that involved eight of Liverpool's nine outfield players and ended with Salah crossing for Gakpo to make it 1-1 with a diving header.

Anfield smelt blood, Fulham were suddenly on the ropes and Gakpo had another shot saved by Bernd Leno. It felt like it was 11v10 in Liverpool's favour.

A Reds counter-attack from a Fulham corner saw Salah fire wide from Szoboszlai's pass before the visitors sent a couple of efforts past Alisson's post and Salah curled another attempt over.

Like a loose horse on a racecourse, you didn't know which way this game was going to go and in the 76th minute Robinson burst into the box and struck a low cross that Rodrigo Muniz converted with a sublime flick of the heel, the ball clipping Gomez on the way in.

Slot sent on Diogo Jota for his long-awaited return from injury, but it was fellow sub, and ex-Fulham player, Harvey Elliott who almost made it 2-2 when he curled one just beyond Leno's post.

Anfield still believed and got their reward in the 86th minute. Gomez found Darwin Nunez, who played a pass into Jota, and with a drop of the shoulder he turned past Jorge Cuenca and sent Leno the wrong way with a low shot into the bottom corner.

The Reds could have won it in stoppage-time when Van Dijk and Diaz had shots blocked in quick succession before Jota's effort was deflected over, but after being a man down for so long it was a point gained.

TOTTENHAM HOTSPUR FC 3
LIVERPOOL FC 6

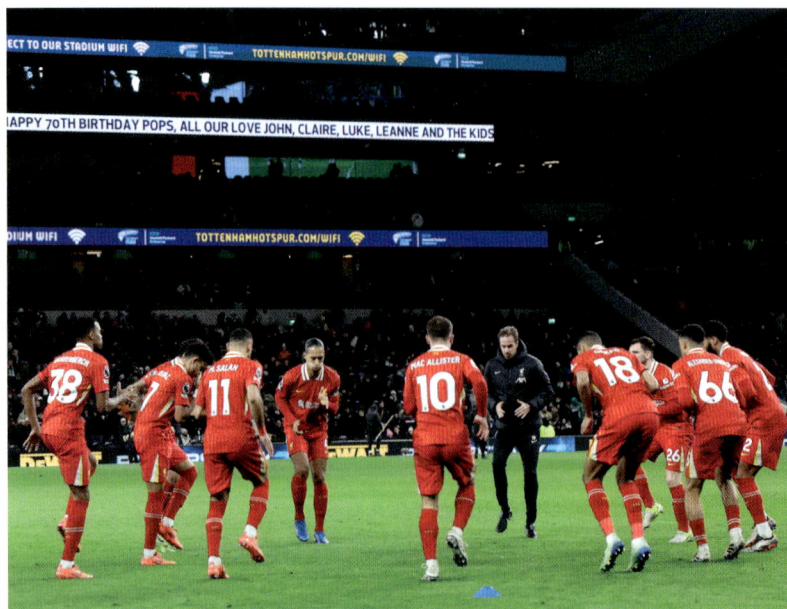

Goals: Diaz (23, 85), Mac Allister (36), Maddison (41), Szoboszlai (45+1), Salah (54, 61), Kulusevski (72), Solanke (83)

22.12.24 · Tottenham Hotspur Stadium

Attendance: 61,439

Referee: Sam Barrott

TOTTENHAM (4-2-3-1): Forster, Porro, Dragusin, Gray, Spence, Sarr (Bergvall 58), Bissouma, Kulusevski, Maddison (Johnson 58), Son (C) (Werner 82), Solanke. Subs not used: Austin, Reguilon, Udogie, Lankshear, Dorrington, Olusesi. Booked: Bergvall.

LIVERPOOL (4-2-3-1): Alisson, Alexander-Arnold, Gomez, Van Dijk (C), Robertson, Gravenberch, Mac Allister (Jones 68), Salah (Elliott 87), Szoboszlai, Gakpo (Jota 68), Diaz (Nunez 87). Subs not used: Kelleher, Endo, Tsimikas, Quansah, Nyoni. Booked: Gakpo, Szoboszlai.

PRESS BOX:
ALYSON RUDD, THE TIMES

"Slot tried to be annoyed at the three goals conceded but admitted that, in the main, he really enjoyed himself. Managers tend to hate games such as this, where both teams are guilty of lapses in concentration and there is an element of pantomime. But you will struggle to find a Liverpool supporter who was at any juncture worried about a Tottenham Hotspur fightback. Indeed, the performance merely underlined that in Slot, the club has a master of timing and rotation."

PUNDIT:
JAMIE CARRAGHER, SKY SPORTS

"Liverpool were excellent today. It felt like a statement performance, a performance of champions elect. It could have been anything today and in some ways the scoreline really flatters Tottenham. It's probably one where the Spurs players have got home and thought 'that could have been worse'."

HEAD COACH:
ARNE SLOT

"Maybe it was our best performance away from home, although I really liked what I saw against Man United as well. Today, apart from scoring six goals, I think we could have even scored more. If you watch the goals one more time back – and that's definitely what I am going to do – it mostly started off with centre-backs or full-backs. Every lead-up to a goal was, I think, multiple passes. So, it's not only the ones that score, it's also the ones that help to create."

FOR THE RECORD:

Mo Salah's second goal took him past Billy Liddell to go fourth on the list of Liverpool's all-time leading goalscorers.

ALSO THIS WEEKEND:

Manchester United 0-3 Bournemouth
Aston Villa 2-1 Manchester City
Brentford 0-2 Nottingham Forest

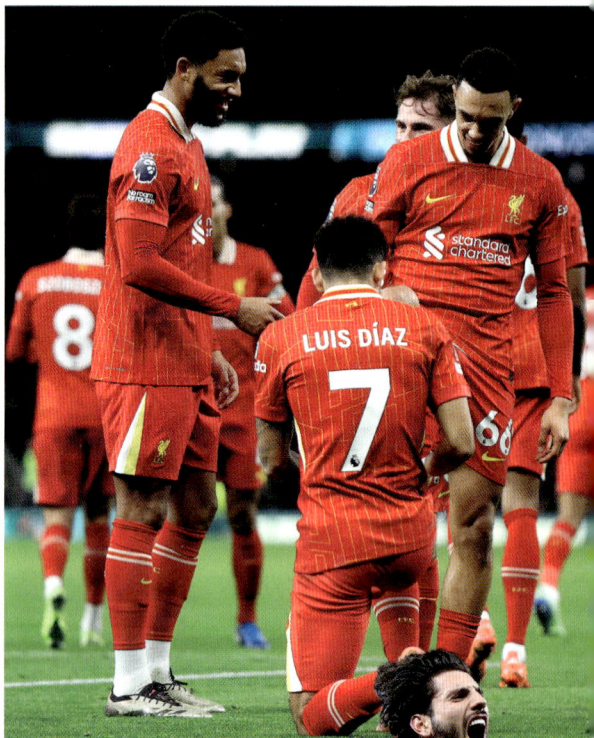

REPORT:

They scored six, but Liverpool could have easily put the ten into Tottenham. The irrepressible Reds missed as many chances as they took in a stunning display of attacking football that carved Spurs open at will.

Only a lack of clinical finishing in some moments and the concession of three goals made the final scoreline look close. It was anything but. Arne Slot's side were sharp, vibrant and exhilarating. Tottenham looked bewildered.

Spurs boss Ange Postecoglou once admitted he grew up following the Reds and must have felt like he could be witnessing a modern-day version of Liverpool's 7-0 thrashing of Tottenham in 1978. In fairness to Postecoglou he had eight players unavailable, but in fairness to Liverpool they'd have won this game had prime Glenn Hoddle and Ossie Ardiles been in the home team. They were magnificent.

Luis Diaz was robbed of a goal on his last visit to the Tottenham Hotspur Stadium due to a VAR debacle – the video official awarding the goal and on-field referee Simon Hooper thinking they'd disallowed it for offside – so it was highly appropriate that he opened the scoring in the 23rd minute.

Trent Alexander-Arnold was given time and space on the right to cultivate a cross that Diaz, playing at centre-forward, met like an uncoiled spring to head past Fraser Forster. Only after glancing towards the assistant referee to see no flag did he celebrate by bending down to polish Trent's boot.

Quite how it was only 1-0 by that point was borderline ridiculous. Mo Salah had hit the side-netting, after being gifted the ball by Forster, forced the Spurs goalie to make a save, had two shots blocked by Djed Spence and struck the crossbar after dribbling past three defenders.

A second goal followed 13 minutes later when Andy Robertson was given so much freedom on the left that you half expected the Mayor of Haringey to walk on and present him with a scroll. Dominik Szoboszlai rose to meet Robertson's cross and the ball flicked off Spence's shoulder for Alexis Mac Allister to dart in and head home.

Spurs got a goal back when Dejan Kulusevski robbed Mac Allister – who felt he was fouled – of possession and slid a pass to James Maddison, who beat Alisson from the edge of the box, but normal service was soon resumed.

Alexander-Arnold clipped the ball forward, Szoboszlai flicked it on for Salah and after running at the Spurs defence he played a reverse pass back to the Hungarian who took a touch before nutmegging Forster with his shot to make it 3-1.

A total Tottenham capitulation looked highly possible early in the second half. Robertson won a challenge, Mac Allister sent Cody Gakpo driving forward and after playing a one-two with Diaz his cross was deflected to Szoboszlai. His shot was blocked on the line by Archie Gray, but Salah was on the premises and didn't miss.

It took Salah to 10 goals and 10 assists before Christmas, the first time in the Premier League that any player has achieved such a feat. Unreal.

Moments later, Alisson clipped a pass forward and Szoboszlai ran clean through from midfield as if he'd been given his own bus lane on the North Circular. He went around Forster, but lost his balance when shooting from a narrow angle and found the side-netting.

The fifth goal arrived soon after. Gakpo played the free-running Szoboszlai in again and he simply squared the ball for Salah to slot it past Forster with consummate ease.

Alexander-Arnold was next to try his luck, Forster diving to his right to palm his shot from 30 yards away, before Diaz had a shot saved.

With the game won the Reds eased up and were reminded that you can't do that in the Premier League as Kulusevski volleyed in Dominic Solanke's chipped pass.

Diaz should have made it six, but lobbed the ball over Forster and the crossbar when played in by Salah, before Spurs got a third, Solanke converting Brennan Johnson's header across goal.

Liverpool flicked the switch back on and Diogo Jota, Szoboszlai and Salah worked the ball to Diaz, who struck a cross-shot beyond Forster to make it 6-3.

It still needed an Alisson save to prevent Johnson from getting another goal back and Lucas Bergvall got an early Christmas present when he wasn't sent off for a foul on Curtis Jones having already been booked, but by then the travelling Kop had long been celebrating the joy of six.

LIVERPOOL FC 3
LEICESTER CITY FC 1

Goals: Ayew (6), Gakpo (45+1), Jones (49), Salah (82)

26.12.24 · Anfield · Attendance: 60,300
Referee: Darren Bond

LIVERPOOL (4-2-3-1): Alisson, Alexander-Arnold, Gomez, Van Dijk (C), Robertson (Tsimikas 86), Gravenberch (Endo 87), Mac Allister (Elliott 90+2), Salah, Jones (Szoboszlai 78), Gakpo, Nunez (Jota 78). Subs not used: Kelleher, Diaz, Chiesa, Quansah. Booked: Gomez, Robertson, Szoboszlai.

LEICESTER (4-2-3-1): Stolarczyk, Justin, Coady (C) (Okoli 90+5), Vestergaard, Kristiansen, Winks (Skipp 65), Soumare, Ayew, El Khannouss (Buonanotte 64), Mavididi (De Cordova-Reid 87), Daka. Subs not used: Iversen, Choudhury, Edouard, Thomas, Alves. Booked: Ayew, Vestergaard.

PRESS BOX:
DAVID ANDERSON, DAILY MIRROR
"It was fitting the fog should partially clear at the final whistle because Liverpool have put daylight between them and the chasing pack in the title race. Arne Slot's side have moved seven points clear at the top of the table – and have a game in hand on their closest challengers Chelsea. This was just as important as Liverpool's 4-0 romp over Leicester on Boxing Day 2019 on their way to their last title, even if it was achieved without the same panache."

PUNDIT:
ALAN SHEARER, BBC MATCH OF THE DAY
"Liverpool are so strong in forward positions and Arne Slot's management of the forward players is really impressive as well. They all look incredibly hungry and when you've got Salah in your side, who is just incredible and keeps going and going, eventually a defence has to break. They just keep going at you until you break. Salah's goal was an outrageous finish. He makes it look so easy, but it's not."

REPORT:

Liverpool started 2024 at Anfield with a 4-2 win against Newcastle United to go three points clear at the top of the Premier League and ended 2024 at Anfield with a 3-1 victory over Leicester City to go seven points clear at the top of the Premier League.

With 23 wins and 78 goals from 28 home matches, it was a top year to watch the Reds on home turf, but they didn't get the job done in 2024.

After this 3-1 win against the Foxes on a foggy Boxing Day night, however, the prospect of 2025 being a top year with a Premier League trophy to show for it increased. The Redmen weren't at their fluent best, à la the 6-3 success at Spurs, but didn't need to be to go seven points ahead in the title race.

Ruud van Nistelrooy's side even led for most of the first half, yet it always felt like Liverpool would find an extra gear when needed. And so they did.

Kopites have enjoyed the festive footy in recent years with the Redmen heading into this game on the back of seven consecutive Boxing Day wins, although never before had they kicked off at 8pm at Anfield on December 26.

The fog gave the game an eerie feel and those at the back of the Anfield Road Stand Upper could've done with Rudolph helping the floodlights to pierce the gloom after ex-Red-turned-Blue Conor Coady made Liverpool attack the Kop end first after winning the toss.

Mo Salah almost opened the scoring in the fifth minute when he

HEAD COACH:
ARNE SLOT

"I think if you're in this game for a long time, like these players are and I am as well, then you know 20 games before the end you don't look at the table. You know so many challenges are still ahead of you. I think it was two months ago we were one point behind [Manchester] City and look what has happened there in terms of injuries and then you have a bit of bad luck, you have a suspension. This can happen to any team, so it's far too early to already be celebrating. But it is of course nice for us to be the team who we are."

FOR THE RECORD:
Liverpool were top of the league on Christmas Day for the 21st time, the most in top-flight history of any club.

ALSO THIS MIDWEEK:
Wolverhampton Wanderers 2-0 Manchester United
Chelsea 1-2 Fulham
Newcastle United 3-0 Aston Villa

volleyed Cody Gakpo's cross against the post before Leicester goalie Jakub Stolarczyk swatted the ball away from Curtis Jones before he could convert the rebound on his 100th league appearance.

Struggling Leicester took a shock lead just a minute later. Stephy Mavididi crossed low from the right and Jordan Ayew controlled the ball and spun Andy Robertson before beating Alisson with a shot on the turn.

Robertson was proving the Reds' best outlet and from a couple of his crosses Darwin Nunez glanced a header wide and forced a corner. A long Robertson pass also got Gakpo in behind James Justin, but after a fantastic first touch the ball got away from him and Stolarczyk smothered.

Salah's deflected effort looped onto the roof of the net and although Trent Alexander-Arnold's corner was cleared he received the ball back and crossed for Robertson, who headed against the inside of the post before the ball ricocheted wide off Stolarczyk.

Leicester's most effective defender was proving to be the woodwork as when Salah curled Alexander-Arnold's pass goalwards the ball kissed the crossbar as if beneath a sprig of mistletoe before bouncing off on its merry way. Seconds later, it was finally in the Foxes' net.

Alexis Mac Allister shifted the ball out to Gakpo on the left, he stepped inside the challenge of Justin and let fly from 19 yards with a curler that left Stolarczyk grasping thick air to put the Reds level just before the interval.

Four minutes after the break, Liverpool led. With Leicester kettled inside their own penalty area and under sustained pressure, Mac Allister got to the byline to pull Salah's pass across goal and Jones arrived on cue to execute a first-time finish.

It made the midfielder the youngest LFC player to score on his 100th Premier League appearance since Michael Owen 24 years prior and the first to mark his century with a goal since Alex Oxlade-Chamberlain... which is a sentence you could have read several times while VAR checked for two offsides before giving the goal.

With the fog thickening, Patson Daka had a chance from another Mavididi cross but mist, sorry, missed his kick under pressure from Virgil van Dijk.

Nunez forced Stolarczyk into a decent stop when he swept Salah's lovely pass goalwards following a flowing move that featured a Gakpo flick and a diagonal pass by Robertson. Gakpo also slammed the ball home when Salah's cross deflected to him, but the edge of Nunez's shoulder was deemed to be offside in the build up after a VAR delay so long you could almost hear revellers singing Auld Lang Syne.

Had the Foxes equalised it would have been a talking point, but instead Salah brought down Gakpo's pass, ran at Victor Kristiansen and bent a shot around the centre-back and into the bottom corner.

Liverpool had ended 2024 at Anfield how they began it – top of the league – and in 2025 they planned to stay there.

WEST HAM UNITED FC 0
LIVERPOOL FC 5

Goals: Diaz (30), Gakpo (40), Salah (44), Alexander-Arnold (54), Jota (84)

29.12.24 · London Stadium
Attendance: 62,476
Referee: Anthony Taylor

WEST HAM (4-2-3-1): Areola, Coufal (Todibo 46), Mavropanos, Kilman, Wan-Bissaka, Paqueta, Alvarez (Fullkrug 46), Kudus (Guilherme 81), Soler (Irving 73), Emerson, Bowen (C) (Summerville 60). Subs not used: Foderingham, Cresswell, Ings, Scarles.

LIVERPOOL (4-2-3-1): Alisson, Alexander-Arnold, Gomez (Quansah 37), Van Dijk (C), Robertson (Tsimikas 74), Gravenberch (Endo 57), Mac Allister, Salah, Jones (Elliott 74), Gakpo (Jota 58), Diaz. Subs not used: Kelleher, Nunez, McConnell, Danns.

PRESS BOX:
LUKE EDWARDS, DAILY TELEGRAPH
"They were irresistible against West Ham and it is starting to look inevitable that Liverpool will be champions. The gap is already large and nothing seems to faze them. We have seen, in the history of sport, teams or individuals who look like they're set to win a gold medal or a league title and have faltered. But the way Liverpool have been under Arne Slot, I just can't see that happening. They're brushing teams away."

PUNDIT:
DANNY MURPHY, BBC MATCH OF THE DAY
"Liverpool have got more players than anybody else who are prepared to run in behind without the ball. They do it with such dynamism it is incredible. It's obviously a tactic and there is a willingness from the players to do it. Mo Salah is probably the best in the Premier League at knowing when to run in behind. He uses his pace, especially when Trent is feeding him. A lot of teams have one, maybe two players, who do it. Liverpool have got four or five and it's impossible to defend."

HEAD COACH:
ARNE SLOT

"Mo and the word 'extraordinary' is something I've heard a lot in the last six months. He truly deserves this and probably for the eight years, but I am involved in the last half-year. I don't think he keeps surprising us because we know what a player he is and we know he is able to do so. Apart from that, he works really hard for the team also when the other team has the ball. We can only hope he can keep bringing these performances in, but I would like to add that if he scores there's also a lead-up to him scoring. So there are also other players that bring him into these positions, but if you bring Mo in these positions, he is extraordinary."

FOR THE RECORD:
Mo Salah became the first player in Liverpool history to score 20 goals for an eighth consecutive season.

ALSO THIS WEEKEND:
Everton 0-2 Nottingham Forest
Leicester City 0-2 Manchester City
Manchester United 0-2 Newcastle United

REPORT:

It is often said that 20-goal-a-season strikers are the most sought after players in football, which makes Liverpool's 20-goal-a-half-season winger truly invaluable.

Two days before 2024 became 2025, Mo Salah reached the 20-goal milestone for an eighth consecutive season as Liverpool demolished West Ham.

Ian Rush scored 20+ goals in nine seasons for LFC, but not consecutively, and he was a no9. Rushie never contributed more than 12 assists in a season either, so for Salah to create his 16th and 17th goals in this 5-0 rout is also remarkable.

The London Stadium hosted superstars such as Usain Bolt, Jessica Ennis-Hill and Mo Farah at the 2012 Olympic Games, but in the decade-plus that has followed it's hard to think of a better player than Salah to have graced the pitch since it became West Ham's home. His 44th-minute goal was his sixth at the venue and his 14th in total against the Hammers. Those goals have come in 11 games, all of which Liverpool have won, and on the evidence of this display the Egyptian King isn't stopping any time soon.

Julen Lopetegui's side were outclassed and could easily have been more than 3-0 down by the half-time interval. Unsurprisingly, it was Salah who had the first chance.

Six minutes had elapsed when Cody Gakpo burst down the left, cut inside and played a diagonal, slide-rule pass that sliced the West Ham defence open. Salah arrived at the far post to strike the ball, but Alphonse Areola dived to his left to make a fine save.

Gakpo narrowly failed to get on the end of a Salah cross shortly afterwards before Liverpool's no11 carved the Hammers open again with an inch-perfect pass for Curtis Jones to run onto and hit, but Areola advanced towards him to block.

Luis Diaz forced the West Ham 'keeper to tip his curling effort over and also headed another opportunity over the crossbar, but the Colombian was becoming increasingly influential and in the 30th minute made it third time lucky.

After running onto Trent Alexander-Arnold's pass he tried to play Jones in, but the ball rebounded back to Diaz off Vladimir Coufal. In the blink of an eye, Diaz dispatched a low, first-time shot past Areola into the bottom corner.

The Reds lost Joe Gomez to injury in the 37th minute and almost lost a goal a minute later. Mohammed Kudus found space between the lines and let fly from 25 yards with a shot that whizzed through Virgil van Dijk's legs, but struck the post.

It was a poke in the Redmen's ribs to remind them a 1-0 lead is always precarious and two minutes later they did something about it. Alexis Mac Allister floated a pass forward, Diaz slipped it inside for Salah and he produced an outrageous flick to spin away from Konstantinos Mavropanos before prodding the ball between Max Kilman's legs for Gakpo to slot home from seven yards out.

Some of the home fans headed for their half-time pie and mash, but another Scouse goal was on the menu. Mac Allister tackled Carlos Soler in his own half, Jones eased a pass to Salah and, on the edge of the box, he stopped the ball almost dead using his studs before clinically whipping a low shot past Areola at his near post. Game over.

Areola prevented Salah getting another in stoppage time and saved from him again two minutes after the restart, but Liverpool weren't declaring at 3-0 and it was Alexander-Arnold who got the fourth. Ryan Gravenberch squared the ball, nobody in a claret and blue shirt attempted to press and Alexander-Arnold didn't need a second invitation to shoot. His effort from 25 yards was goalbound, but clipped Kilman to wrongfoot Areola on the way in.

Alexander-Arnold burst through midfield unchallenged again in the 66th minute and found Salah, but this time he curled his effort wide. Shortly after, Wataru Endo, on for Gravenberch, won possession and found Salah. His cross was punched out to another Reds sub, Diogo Jota, but Areola repelled his goalbound effort.

Kudus headed against the bar, albeit with the offside flag up, in a rare Hammers attack before Jota made it 5-0. Endo won the ball again, Salah drove forward down the centre of the pitch and Jota expertly curled his pass into the top corner.

Many West Ham fans had long gone home, but won't have been surprised to hear that Liverpool's 20-goal-a-half-season winger had undone them again. What a player. What a season.

REPORT:

Liverpool and Manchester are very different cities, but on the morning of this clash between the Reds and Red Devils they looked very much the same – covered in snow.

Only when the Anfield pitch was cleared, surrounding areas checked and travel issues assessed did this 216th meeting of England's most successful clubs get the go-ahead.

In truth, it suited Manchester United more than Liverpool. Playing at Anfield for the first time under the management of Ruben Amorim, United arrived on Merseyside 23 points behind the Redmen and on the back of three consecutive defeats in which they'd failed to score. Another loss would make it their worst run since 1979.

Amorim had evidently realised his team couldn't out-football Arne Slot's Premier League leaders so adopted a more direct style. Every goal kick was launched downfield by Andre Onana like he was an angry neighbour sick of finding next door's football in his garden. If United got a free-kick pretty much anywhere on the pitch it was lofted into the Liverpool penalty area.

It wasn't what you'd expect to see from Manchester United but on a heavy, rain-sodden pitch which visibly slowed the ball, and amidst the relentless freezing sleet that gave supporters a soaking on the way to the ground, it worked. The game flowed, but Liverpool weren't quite as their slickest and United made it a contest.

Fifteen minutes had been played before either side created a

LIVERPOOL FC 2
MANCHESTER UNITED FC 2

Goals: Martinez (52), Gakpo (59), Salah (70pen), Diallo (80)

05.01.25 · Anfield · Attendance: 60,275

Referee: Michael Oliver

LIVERPOOL (4-2-3-1): Alisson, Alexander-Arnold (Bradley 86), Konate, Van Dijk (C), Robertson, Gravenberch, Mac Allister, Salah, Jones (Jota 61), Gakpo (Elliott 86), Diaz (Nunez 60). Subs not used: Kelleher, Endo, Chiesa, Tsimikas, Quansah. Booked: Nunez, Alexander-Arnold.

MANCHESTER UNITED (3-4-2-1): Onana, De Ligt (Yoro 83), Maguire, Martinez, Mazraoui, Ugarte, Mainoo (Garnacho 72), Dalot, Diallo, Fernandes (C), Højlund (Zirkzee 86). Subs not used: Bayindir, Malacia, Eriksen, Casemiro, Antony, Collyer. Booked: Dalot, Diallo, De Ligt, Maguire.

PRESS BOX:

PAUL GORST, LIVERPOOL ECHO

"Having entered football's most-watched club fixture 23 points clear of their arch-rivals, Liverpool failed to showcase their superiority as a much-improved United halted a run of four successive defeats at the most unlikely venue of them all. The opportunity to carve open more breathing space at the summit was instead spurned, handing a lifeline to Arsenal, who are now six points adrift of the Reds having played a game more than Slot's team."

PUNDIT:

JAMIE CARRAGHER, SKY SPORTS

"It was a little lesson for Liverpool. The players maybe got a bit carried away by how poor United were on Monday. Anfield is at its best is when it's energetic. There wasn't one time in the first half when United had the ball and Liverpool went and won it, and the crowd got up. The big worry for me is Liverpool are starting to concede goals. They have more goals and attacking talent than Arsenal, but if you were Arsenal watching that, I'd be enthused."

HEAD COACH:

ARNE SLOT

"It feels for us as two points dropped. In the end, it was a difficult game. A bit similar to maybe the Nottingham Forest game, where the playing style of both teams was quite similar. Defending in a low block with a lot of bodies and if they had the ball, not the risk of build-up, but play it long. Every free-kick they got somewhere in and around their own half or our half, they brought it in, so that was a bit similar to Forest. That is not always easy then to play against that style of football and that's what showed against Forest and it showed again today."

FOR THE RECORD:

Mo Salah's goal was his 16th against Man United and means only Ian Rush (25 v Everton) and Gordon Hodgson (17 v Derby County) have scored more for Liverpool against one opponent.

ALSO THIS WEEKEND:

Brighton & Hove Albion 1-1 Arsenal
Crystal Palace 1-1 Chelsea
Wolves 0-3 Nottingham Forest

notable chance and it was Cody Gakpo who had it. Luis Diaz found Ryan Gravenberch with a reverse pass and he slipped the ball to his fellow Dutchman who dinked a shot over the advancing Onana, but it dropped wide of the far post.

Moments later, Virgil van Dijk sprayed a pass out wide to Mo Salah and he clipped a ball into the box that the forward-running Alexis Mac Allister met on the half-volley, but Onana blocked with his shin. Slot put his hands on his head in frustration.

Diogo Dalot went into the book for mistakenly thinking he was in a greco-roman wrestling contest with Salah before Gravenberch burst past Kobbie Mainoo and sent a venomous low shot past the post.

The visitors finally tested Alisson in the 43rd minute when Rasmus Hojlund ran into space behind Trent Alexander-Arnold and got a shot away, but the Reds' goalie made himself big and blocked with his chest.

Early in the second stanza, Van Dijk blocked Dalot's shot with a perfectly-timed sliding challenge, but United were starting to threaten and took the lead in the 52nd minute. Lisandro Martinez, forward from a previous phase of play, was found by Bruno Fernandes and he smashed the ball in off the underside of the crossbar. It was only the second goal the Red Devils had scored at Anfield since January 2016.

United's lead lasted just seven minutes. Mac Allister slid a pass to Gakpo, who left his Dutch international teammate Matthijs de Ligt sliding towards the Kop as he turned the ball back onto his right foot and rifled a shot past Onana.

A VAR check for offside didn't save United and De Ligt's afternoon got worse when, just moments after being booked for fouling substitute Darwin Nunez, he raised his arm to block Mac Allister's header in the penalty area. To Anfield's incredulity, referee Michael Oliver played on, but was soon summoned to the pitchside monitor and belatedly pointed to the spot. Salah stepped up and slotted home his 16th goal in 17 games against United, a phenomenal record.

He almost made it 17 when, after being chopped down by Harry Maguire on the edge of the penalty area, he whipped a free-kick just over the bar with Onana rooted.

Nunez risked a red card when catching De Ligt with his arm and, although it felt like a Liverpool win would follow, this fixture has a history of results belying league positions and the visitors equalised with 10 minutes to play. Alejandro Garnacho pulled the ball back and Amad Diallo scuffed a shot beyond Alisson.

Both sides had chances to win it. Alisson saved from Fernandes before a Reds counter-attack ended with Onana beating out a Diogo Jota effort and stopping Conor Bradley from embarrassing him at his near post.

From Andy Robertson's corner, Van Dijk headed Mac Allister's flick-on straight at Onana and down the other end Maguire had a gilt-edged opportunity to snatch three points, but scooped Joshua Zirkzee's pass over from 10 yards out.

The only winner was the weather.

NOTTINGHAM FOREST FC 1
LIVERPOOL FC 1

Goals: Wood (8), Jota (66)
14.01.25 · City Ground
Attendance: 30,249
Referee: Chris Kavanagh

NOTTINGHAM FOREST (4-2-3-1): Sels, Aina, Milenkovic, Murillo, Williams (Moreno 90), Yates (C), (Dominguez 76), Anderson, Elanga, Gibbs-White (Morato 90), Hudson-Odoi (Jota Silva 83), Wood (Awoniyi 90). Subs not used: Miguel, Boly, Ward-Prowse, Sosa. Booked: Gibbs-White, Yates.

LIVERPOOL (4-3-3): Alisson, Alexander-Arnold, Konate (Jota 66), Van Dijk (C), Robertson (Tsimkas 66), Gravenberch, Mac Allister, Szoboszlai, Salah, Diaz (Jones 75), Gakpo. Subs not used: Kelleher, Endo, Chiesa, Elliott, Quansah, Bradley. Booked: Diaz.

PRESS BOX:
IAN LADYMAN, DAILY MAIL

"By the end Forest were hanging on, clinging to imaginary branches as a Liverpool tidal wave washed over them. By full-time, their goalkeeper Matz Sels had announced himself as their best player. But at the same time this was a scare for Liverpool. Forest's rope-a-dope tactics had bounced them into an early lead as their centre forward Chris Wood broke away to score. Liverpool, the league leaders, were rattled. They were unsure and anxious. Lots and lots of possession – 71 per cent of it by full-time – but for the first hour at least not a single shot on target."

PUNDIT:
MICHAEL OWEN, PREMIER LEAGUE MATCHDAY LIVE

"I don't think I've ever seen that before. I've seen someone come on and score with their first touch within seconds, but for a double substitution – a cross to come from one and a header to come into the back of the net from the other – is quite incredible. What an impact. What a substitution!"

HEAD COACH:
ARNE SLOT

"With how the game went, I think we can be disappointed. They are a counter-attacking team and I think we only conceded one counter-attack – and for us to come from behind shows the character and quality the team has. Our fans, our players and me, we want to win the league, but we want the fans to come and see us and like what they see. We played some outstanding football in the second half. Maybe the intensity was a little bit higher, but maybe the other team is a little bit more tired too."

FOR THE RECORD:
Diogo Jota scored 21 seconds after he came on, equalling the record for the shortest time taken by a Liverpool player to score set by David Thompson (v Southampton in 1999) and Daniel Sturridge (v West Ham in 2018).

ALSO THIS MIDWEEK:
Brentford 2-2 Manchester City
Everton 0-1 Aston Villa
Chelsea 2-2 Bournemouth

REPORT:

"We're in your head, in your heaaaad, Arne, Arne, Arne-e-e," chanted the Nottingham Forest fans.

Having become the only side to beat Slot's Liverpool in the Premier League, the home supporters evidently thought they'd been on Slot's mind for four months, but when this pulsating clash ended even a zombie would have seen the Reds should have won.

Sluggish in the first half, they turned in the best 45 minutes any Liverpool side has conjured up at the City Ground – a long-time bogey ground – in living memory after the break, but were denied a comeback win by some incredible defending and goalkeeping.

Brazilian centre-back Murillo made 18 clearances, the most by any player in the Premier League all season. His central defensive partner Nikola Milenkovic completed 12 of the 59 clearances Forest made in total.

Goalkeeper Matz Sels left the pitch with five saves to his name. Quite simply, they held on.

Backed by a noisy, partisan support, it was a show of defensive resilience that, just about, prevented Slot's men from getting the three points their second-half showing warranted.

Liverpool started on the front-foot. Alexis Mac Allister had a shot blocked, Cody Gakpo curled wide, Ryan Gravenberch fired Mo Salah's

pull-back over. But in the ninth minute they were caught cold by arguably the best counter-attacking team in the division.

Ibrahima Konate moved out of the backline to head clear, but Salah was tackled by Callum Hudson-Odoi. In the blink of an eye, Anthony Elanga slipped a pass into the space Konate had vacated for Chris Wood and he beat Alisson with a low, first-time cross-shot that snuck inside the far post like an outlaw giving a sheriff the slip.

It was an unsettling setback in Liverpool's chase to wear the Premier League's gold badge. Nuno Espirito Santo's side had their tails up and moments later Murillo fizzed a swerving long-range effort wide.

The Reds created half-chances. Gakpo headed a Salah cross wide, Dominik Szoboszlai's header was blocked by Anfield alumni Neco Williams and Mac Allister saw an attempt deflect past the post. Luis Diaz, running onto a sublime Trent Alexander-Arnold pass, also missed the chance to play Gakpo clean through when he took an extra touch and Murillo was able to intercept.

Of nine first-half shots, none were on target, but Liverpool were kicking towards the travelling Kop in the Bridgford Stand when play resumed and completely dominated.

Salah scuffed a shot wide, but Alexander-Arnold had to survive a VAR check for serious foul play when he tried to punch the ball

towards where Forest had been awarded a free-kick, but inadvertently clocked Elliot Anderson in the face instead. VAR deemed it accidental and Alisson beat Elanga's free-kick away at his near post.

When Williams conceded a 66th-minute corner, Slot opted to introduce substitutes Kostas Tsimikas and Diogo Jota for Andy Robertson and Konate before it was taken. It was an inspired move.

Tsimikas delivered the corner and Jota, just 21 seconds after entering the fray, rose at the far post to glance home an equaliser. For two players to assist and score with their first touches was remarkable.

Jota was on a mission to win the game by himself and when he latched onto a Salah pass and sent Murillo for an Echo with a deft turn, only Sels stood between the Portuguese and the goal, but the big Belgian made a good stop.

He was at it again in the 77th minute. Alexander-Arnold's cross was diverted to Jota and as he struck a half-volley goalwards Sels flew out to deflect the shot with his knee against the knee of Ola Aina, on the goalline, and the ball ricocheted clear. When your luck is in and all that.

Salah had a penalty claim turned down after being sandwiched by Williams and Anderson before Sels touched Szoboszlai's daisy-cutter wide. The Egyptian also skied another opportunity.

Liverpool continued to press and when Salah got another curled

effort right, Sels dived to his right to punch over. From Alexander-Arnold's corner, the ball was diverted to Salah, but Aina was like an additional Forest goalpost and blocked on the line for the second time.

When Sels got down to his left in stoppage-time to tip Gakpo's effort past the upright, Slot laughed knowingly. It wasn't going to happen, but were Forest's fans in his heaaaad?

"I thought they maybe just liked the style of play my team had," he quipped. "We created chance after chance after chance..."

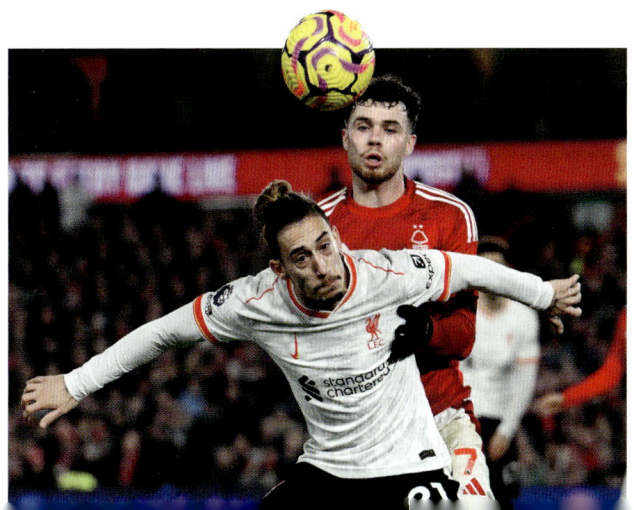

BRENTFORD FC 0
LIVERPOOL FC 2

Goals: Nunez (90+1, 90+3)

18.01.25 · Gtech Community Stadium

Attendance: 17,215

Referee: Andy Madley

BRENTFORD (4-2-3-1): Flekken, Roerslev, Collins, Van den Berg, Lewis-Potter, Norgaard (C), Janelt (Schade 66), Mbeumo, Damsgaard (Jensen 81), Yarmoliuk, Wissa. Subs not used: Valdimarsson, Henry, Carvalho, Mee, Kokak, Kim, Maghoma. Booked: Norgaard, Roerslev.

LIVERPOOL (4-2-3-1): Alisson, Alexander-Arnold, Konate, Van Dijk (C), Tsimikas (Robertson 65), Gravenberch, Mac Allister (Jones 80), Salah, Szoboszlai (Elliott 80), Gakpo (Chiesa 87), Diaz (Nunez 65). Subs not used: Kelleher, Endo, Quansah, Bradley. Booked: Tsimikas, Szoboszlai, Nunez.

PRESS BOX:

PAUL GORST, LIVERPOOL ECHO

"Liverpool's 2-0 win here was a triumph of persistence. The winning goals came via shots 36 and 37 and while goalkeeper Mark Flekken was not forced to do anything extraordinary for any of those, there can be ultimately few complaints from the hosts that they ended this one pointless. It's the most shots an away side has had in recorded history, which dates back 22 years, and no other player in the Premier League's 33 years has scored more winning goals in stoppage time than Nunez's three now either."

PUNDIT:

NIGEL SPACKMAN, LFCTV

"Coming off the bench, that's what you're supposed to do – make an impact. Liverpool were missing Jota so someone else had to step up. Darwin came off the bench and was in the right place at the right time. The first one showed a striker's instinct and all the Liverpool supporters erupted. This is a massive, massive win today."

BRENTFORD FC v LIVERPOOL FC

HEAD COACH:
ARNE SLOT

"We were close to not getting what we deserved. The amount of chances we created was like on Tuesday against Forest – a lot. We were close to going off without a win. That combined with a late winner is what we were most happy about. And it was a significant game. I don't only look at results. We created a lot. But now it's a win so I don't have to say look at our performance. I was very pleased with our performance."

FOR THE RECORD:
Darwin Nunez became the second Liverpool substitute to score twice in a 2-0 win following David Fairclough against Burnley in 1976.

ALSO THIS WEEKEND:
Arsenal 2-2 Aston Villa
Newcastle United 1-4 Bournemouth
Manchester United 1-3 Brighton & Hove Albion

REPORT:

You can't win a Premier League title without a bit of late drama along the way.

In 2019/20 it was Andy Robertson and Sadio Mane who secured a last-ditch win at Villa Park at a crucial juncture of the season. In 2024/25 it was Darwin Nunez at the Gtech Community Stadium.

Having dropped points in their opening two games of 2025 it looked like Liverpool would be held by Brentford despite having mustered 35 attempts on goal as the clock ticked into stoppage-time. But cometh the 91st minute, cometh La Pantera, as they say in Uruguay.

On as a 65th-minute substitute, the Brentford fans had taunted Nunez with unfavourable comparisons to Andy Carroll, but when Liverpool's no9 pounced, like the black cat he is nicknamed after, to put the Reds ahead they weren't miaowing any more. And when Nunez added a quick-fire second it had travelling Kopites roaring.

Although it had looked like being one of those days when the Bees' goal had a forcefield preventing the ball from entering it until Nunez intervened, Brentford boss Thomas Frank was effusive with his praise for Arne Slot's Reds.

"We just played City and Arsenal and now Liverpool, in a short amount of time – for me they're a level above those two teams. They're complete. Their work ethic, the way they track back. They're so good all over the pitch. Such a threat going forward. These are really good. It's the best team in the Premier League and the world."

Nice to hear, but had Mikkel Damsgaard not completely missed Mads Roerslev's deflected cross, from four yards out in front of an open goal, early in the first half the best team in the world would have been a goal down.

Liverpool dominated possession and Brentford retreated into a 5-5-0 formation with Bryan Mbeumo, singled out by Slot to his players in his pre-match analysis, dropping into an unfamiliar right-sided midfield role to keep tabs on Kostas Tsimikas.

Even so, the Redmen created plenty of chances. Cody Gakpo headed straight at Mark Flekken, Ryan Gravenberch forced the Bees' goalie to turn his 25-yard effort past the post and Dominik Szoboszlai didn't get enough power on his shot after a mazy run.

That wasn't the case moments later when Szoboszlai let fly from 25 yards with a powerful drive that struck the crossbar.

At the other end, Virgil van Dijk and Ibrahima Konate were dealing with Brentford's physicality admirably and an interception by the Reds' skipper in his own six-yard box began a flowing, end-to-end counter-attack that led to Gakpo clipping Mo Salah's cross past Flekken, but also the post.

Liverpool spent so much of the second period camped in the Brentford half that they could have lit a fire and gathered around it to sing songs, but they couldn't find a goal.

Szoboszlai, Salah and Luis Diaz had shots blocked and Diaz also fired wide. In the 63rd minute, Gravenberch found the Colombian with a delightful pass and after Flekken saved his shot he pushed it back towards Diaz, who went down as the Dutchman stretched out an arm, but the contact was minimal.

On came Robertson and Nunez, and just two minutes later the pair combined to create a chance, but the Uruguayan misdirected his header wide.

Alexis Mac Allister had a couple of shots blocked in quick succession and also headed a Robertson corner into the side-netting before Alisson was finally called into action to make routine saves from Mbeumo, Kevin Schade and Yoane Wissa.

Trent Alexander-Arnold lashed a 30-yarder just past the upright with Flekken at full-stretch and Salah bent a shot narrowly wide.

Having already introduced Curtis Jones and Harvey Elliott, Slot made his final roll of the dice with Federico Chiesa coming on in the 87th minute. Four minutes later, the Italian was celebrating wildly in front of the Liverpool supporters when Nunez broke the deadlock.

Elliott cleverly played Alexander-Arnold in and although his first cross was blocked, he instantly struck the ball across goal and Nunez tucked it home from six yards before ripping off his shirt and running to the delirious travelling Kop.

The celebrations were still going when Salah won a challenge, Chiesa drove forward, Elliott took it on and found Nunez, who took a touch before rifling into the roof of the net to seal a dramatic first Premier League win of 2025.

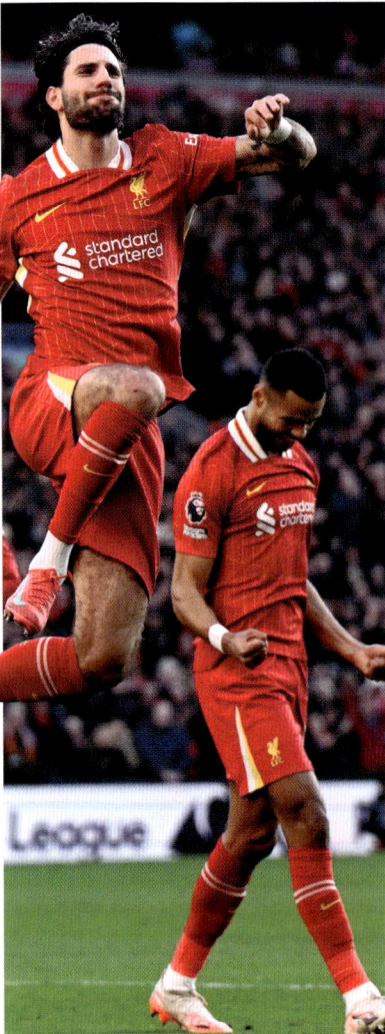

LIVERPOOL FC v IPSWICH TOWN FC

REPORT:

When Liverpool were two games shy of winning a historic quadruple in May 2022, Ipswich Town were finishing 11th in League One, a place above Accrington Stanley.

So to be at Anfield playing in the Premier League just two-and-a-half years later was a success in itself and testament to the job Kieran McKenna has done at Portman Road. However, the scale of the task facing the Tractor Boys was laid bare in one single statistic.

They arrived on Merseyside having scored 20 goals in 22 games. Mo Salah had scored 18, having played a game less, and needed just one to make it a century of league goals for Liverpool at Anfield. There are levels and there are levels.

Ipswich had won two of their three previous visits to Anfield, but the most recent one,

in 2002, was a 5-0 defeat that saw them relegated. Arne Slot's class of 2024/25 weren't far off repeating that scoreline.

Virgil van Dijk made his 300th appearance and with Ibrahima Konate also in good form the Ipswich attack would've got more change from a broken vending machine. Until the final moments, Alisson was a spectator and Liverpool had the points in the bag by half-time.

Beaten 6-0 at home to Manchester City in their previous outing, the visitors tried to park the combine harvester in an attempt to prevent a similar scoreline, but when Cody Gakpo cut inside and fired over in the first minute it was quickly evident that the Reds meant business.

Ten minutes later, the deadlock was broken. Van Dijk played a pass across to Konate, who was allowed to bring it forward into the Ipswich

LIVERPOOL FC 4
IPSWICH TOWN FC 1

Goals: Szoboszlai (11), Salah (35), Gakpo (44, 65), Greaves (90)

25.01.25 · Anfield · Attendance: 60,420
Referee: Michael Salisbury

LIVERPOOL (4-2-3-1): Alisson, Alexander-Arnold, Konate, Van Dijk (C), Robertson, Gravenberch (Endo 68), Mac Allister (Danns 80), Salah, Szoboszlai (Elliott 68), Diaz (Chiesa 86), Gakpo (Nunez 68). Subs not used: Kelleher, Tsimikas, Quansah, Bradley.

IPSWICH (4-2-3-1): Walton, Tuanzebe, O'Shea, Greaves, Davis (Townsend 46), Morsy (C), Phillips, Burns (Johnson 29), Hutchinson (Enciso 79), Philogene (Broadhead 79), Delap (Hirst 79). Subs not used: Muric, Taylor, Luongo, Godfrey. Booked: Delap, Enciso.

PRESS BOX:
JOE BERNSTEIN, DAILY MAIL

"What separates Liverpool from their title rivals is the range of firepower available to Arne Slot. With last week's two-goal hero Darwin Nunez restricted to the bench, this was Cody Gakpo's time to weigh in with a brace, quite besides the Premier League's top scorer Mo Salah taking his season's tally to 23 in all competitions. It's the main reason that Liverpool are spending the first anniversary of Jürgen Klopp's bombshell departure announcement six points clear at the top of the table with a game in hand."

PUNDIT:
**DANNY MURPHY,
BBC MATCH OF THE DAY**

"I've eulogised in recent weeks about Liverpool's forward players and the creativity, dynamism and depth, but I think the bedrock of their success is the centre-halves in Van Dijk and Konate and Gravenberch just in front, which has been a masterstroke from Arne Slot. I think if you want to be a Premier League title winner you need your centre-halves to play good football and Konate is undervalued in that respect."

HEAD COACH: ARNE SLOT

"I think today is the way you want to start the game: we were aggressive, dominant. For 85 minutes they have hardly been in our half. It is a counter-attack threat with the wingers they have and with [Liam] Delap, but we managed to control that so, so, so well because of the amount of work we have put in. In the end, we are all a bit disappointed with conceding from a corner – the first one this season – but for 85 minutes it was almost a perfect performance, against a team that goes to such a low block. That's not always easy, but the way we did it for 85 minutes was really good."

FOR THE RECORD:
The crowd of 60,420 was a new record for a league fixture at Anfield.

ALSO THIS WEEKEND:
Manchester City 3-1 Chelsea
Wolverhampton Wanderers 0-1 Arsenal
Bournemouth 5-0 Nottingham Forest

half. He found Dominik Szoboszlai, in space between the lines, and after turning the ball back onto his left foot to get away from Jacob Greaves he struck a low shot from 20 yards that Christian Walton could only push into the bottom corner.

Alexis Mac Allister was the next to try his luck from distance, but dragged an effort from almost 30 yards wide of the post before the visitors lost Wes Burns to a serious looking injury that was later confirmed to be a season-ending torn ACL.

When play resumed, Salah had a shot – again created by a Konate pass – blocked, but in the 33rd minute he could've raised his bat after reaching a century of Premier League goals on home turf.

Gakpo again cut inside from the left, but this time delivered a cross to the far post that Salah brought down on his right thigh before smashing the ball into the roof of the net with his trusty left foot.

The fact that Slot could field his strongest available XI between matchdays seven and eight of the revamped Champions League was testament to how well the Reds had done in Europe, qualifying with maximum points ahead of a trip to PSV. Ipswich must have wished the Liverpool head coach had rested players here, not in Eindhoven, as by half-time it was 3-0.

Mac Allister intercepted a pass and found Ryan Gravenberch, who played an incisive ball behind the Ipswich defence for Szoboszlai to strike first-time while on the run. Walton got down to save, but Gakpo was on hand to snaffle the rebound. The visitors appealed for offside, but with their back four in a diagonal line Axel Tuanzebe was playing Szoboszlai miles on and the goal stood.

Szoboszlai almost curled home another on the stroke of half-time and the only surprise was that the second half finished 1-1. Liverpool's fourth goal came in the 66th minute when Trent Alexander-Arnold curled a cross to the far post so perfectly that Gakpo barely had to nod to head it in from six yards.

A fifth goal simply wouldn't come. Harvey Elliott sliced a shot past one post, Alexander-Arnold whistled an effort past the other. He came even closer in the 78th minute when Wataru Endo touched Salah's pass to him, but his right-footed strike hit the inside of the upright.

The Reds eased up in the final five minutes and after Alisson made a superb save to claw away a George Hirst header, Greaves got a goal back in the 90th minute when he jumped between Elliott and Jayden Danns to head in a corner.

It was a nice moment for the Ipswich fans who, three years ago to the day, were watching their team at AFC Wimbledon, but for Liverpool it was merely a slight blemish on a routine win.

AFC BOURNEMOUTH 0
LIVERPOOL FC 2

Goals: Salah (30pen, 75)
01.02.25 · Vitality Stadium
Attendance: 11,239
Referee: Darren England

BOURNEMOUTH (4-2-3-1): Arrizabalaga, Cook (C), Zabarnyi, Huijsen, Kerkez, Christie (Jebbison 80), Adams, Brooks (Tavernier 66), Kluivert, Semenyo, Ouattara. Subs not used: Dennis, Silcott-Duberry, Adu-Adjei, Akinmboni, Winterburn, Kinsey, Rees-Dottin. Booked: Christie, Huijsen.

LIVERPOOL (4-2-3-1): Alisson, Alexander-Arnold (Bradley 70), Konate, Van Dijk (C), Robertson, Gravenberch, Mac Allister (Jones 61), Salah (Endo 88), Szoboszlai, Gakpo (Nunez 70), Diaz. Subs not used: Kelleher, Jota, Tsimikas, Elliott, Quansah. Booked: Gravenberch, Mac Allister, Van Dijk.

AFC BOURNEMOUTH v LIVERPOOL FC

PRESS BOX:
JOHN BREWIN, THE GUARDIAN
"Liverpool marched on, though with no little relief, their post-match celebrations reflecting the importance of victory. Arne Slot's team had not triggered the traps Andoni Iraola's Bournemouth had used to snare the top-four contenders Manchester City, Arsenal and Nottingham Forest this season. It was Mohamed Salah who snatched the three points. If his first came after a highly debatable penalty award, the second, a left-foot chip like a prime Tiger Woods approach shot, was a goal of inarguable beauty."

PUNDIT:
NEIL MELLOR, LFCTV
"It felt like a big win. We went to Brentford a couple of weeks ago and that was a really important win, but this feels bigger. What a season Ryan Gravenberch is having, another top display again. His numbers were incredible during the game and he also ran 10.4km. Curtis Jones was absolutely magnificent for the second goal. He started the move on the edge of his own box and then sprinted forward to provide the assist, and Salah did what he does."

HEAD COACH:
ARNE SLOT
"If you want to win here against a team that is so competitive then you need a team performance and work-rate. That's what we have and you need some quality individuals that make the difference for you and that goal of Mo was absolute quality and the saves Alisson made as well. But it was not only them, the way our centre-backs were defending again today was also impressive."

FOR THE RECORD:
Mo Salah made it five top-flight seasons in which he has scored 20+ goals for LFC. Only Gordon Hodgson (seven) has scored 20+ in more.

ALSO THIS WEEKEND:
Arsenal 5-1 Manchester City
Manchester United 0-2 Crystal Palace
Nottingham Forest 7-0 Brighton

REPORT:
There are wins, and there are big wins in a Premier League title race. This was a big win for Liverpool.

Unbeaten in 12 Premier League games, Bournemouth had already beaten Arsenal, Manchester City and Nottingham Forest at the Vitality Stadium. No team had won more often since the end of November and despite losing 3-0 at Anfield earlier in the season, Andoni Iraola's side had 19 shots on goal, won nine corners and forced Alisson into seven saves.

The size and history of the respective clubs will always mean that Liverpool are expected to beat Bournemouth, but under the Spaniard they have developed into a team capable of playing exciting, attacking football and are in the hunt for European qualification for the first time in their history.

So if anyone wrongly thought the Reds would stroll to three points beside the seaside they needed to wait just 12 seconds for a reality check. Ryan Gravenberch kicked off, Alexis Mac Allister played the ball back to Trent Alexander-Arnold, who was immediately pressed and tackled by Antoine Semenyo.

The Ghanaian international drove forward, cut back inside Alexander-Arnold and hit a low shot that Alisson had to dive to his right to save.

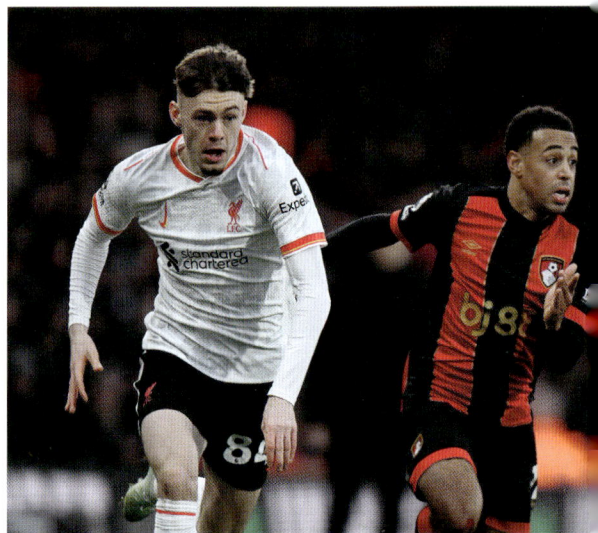

Liverpool heeded the warning and within a minute Luis Diaz forced a corner. Andy Robertson sent in an outswinger, the ball ricocheted to Diaz and the Colombian looked set to score from four yards until Dean Huijsen slid in to make a goal-saving challenge.

It set the tone for a match that had 33 shots on goal. Justin Kluivert forced Alisson to save at his near post following Alexander-Arnold's mis-timed clearance before Cody Gakpo shook off the attention of two defenders to cut inside and blast goalwards, Kepa Arrizabalaga diving to his right to save.

Three minutes later the lively Semenyo beat Alexander-Arnold again before getting away from Ibrahima Konate and unleashing a powerful drive that flashed past Alisson, but clattered the inside of the post.

He didn't have it all his own way though and when Gravenberch dispossessed Semenyo the Reds launched a flowing counter-attack that ended with Gakpo playing Dominik Szoboszlai in only for Kepa to repel his shot.

Quite how it was still 0-0 was a bigger mystery than how Linda survived seven episodes of The Traitors before being uncloaked, but the goalless scoreline was banished in the 27th minute.

Gakpo chased after Robertson's long pass and, as he sized up a shot on goal, was tripped by Lewis Cook inside the penalty area. Referee

Darren England pointed to the spot and the faithful Salah slotted the spot-kick low to Kepa's left.

The Cherries thought they'd equalised 10 minutes later when the overlapping Milos Kerkez crossed for David Brooks to slam home, but the Hungarian left-back was offside.

Still the chances came. Diaz had a header saved, as did Alexander-Arnold when he arrived at pace to meet Salah's cross, before Szoboszlai lifted a shot over while challenged by Semenyo.

Bournemouth started the second half like the first, Dango Ouattara heading over 15 seconds after kick-off. Moments later, Kluivert's volley was blocked by Konate before Alisson darted off his line to prevent Semenyo from equalising after being played in by Ryan Christie.

Arne Slot introduced Curtis Jones followed by Darwin Nunez and Conor Bradley – replacing the injured Alexander-Arnold – and the changes helped Liverpool to wrestle control of the game, but only after a massive scare.

Cherries substitute Marcus Tavernier beat Alisson with a curler that hit the inside of the post. The rebound fell to Kluivert, six yards out with the goal at his mercy, but he inexplicably shanked the ball into the stand. It was a sitter.

Bradley had a shot blocked before the game's defining moment occurred in the 75th minute. Jones intercepted a pass on the edge of his own box and after Nunez and Diaz counter-attacked the Scouse midfielder arrived on the edge of the Bournemouth box to slip the ball to Salah, who took a touch before almost nonchalantly clipping a curling shot around Kerkez and beyond Kepa, who didn't even dive. Pure class.

Semenyo hadn't given up. He fizzed a shot just past Alisson's post that knocked over a camera behind the goal before Alisson made perhaps his best reaction save of the season so far when he got down low to palm the ball away after Semenyo beat Bradley and fired in a cross that Gravenberch deflected towards his own goal.

Maybe Bournemouth deserved more, but this was a big win for Liverpool.

EVERTON FC 2
LIVERPOOL FC 2

Goals: Beto (11), Mac Allister (16), Salah (73), Tarkowski (90+8)

12.02.25 · Goodison Park
Attendance: 39,280
Referee: Michael Oliver

EVERTON (4-2-3-1): Pickford, O'Brien, Tarkowski (C), Branthwaite, Mykolenko, Garner (Young 87), Gueye (Iroegbunam 77), Lindstrom (Alcaraz 77), Doucoure, Ndiaye (Harrison 25), Beto. Subs not used: Virginia, Begovic, Keane, Sherif, Heath. Booked: Lindstrom, Gueye, Doucoure. Sent off: Doucoure (90+14).

LIVERPOOL (4-2-3-1): Alisson, Bradley (Jones 61), Konate, Van Dijk (C), Robertson (Tsimikas 79), Gravenberch (Alexander-Arnold 61), Mac Allister, Salah, Szoboszlai, Gakpo (Nunez 79), Diaz (Jota 88). Subs not used: Kelleher, Endo, Elliott, Quansah. Booked: Robertson, Bradley, Jones. Sent-off: Jones (90+13), Slot, Hulshoff.

PRESS BOX:
RICHARD JOLLY, THE INDEPENDENT
"Liverpool felt the equaliser should have been chalked off, that Beto had fouled Konate. Everton enjoyed Tarkowski's glorious goal. Cue the red cards, the red mist. Goodison's final derby and its last night game showed the magic of the old place. Bramley-Moore Dock has quite a lot to live up to."

PUNDIT:
STEVE McMANAMAN, TNT SPORTS
"It was only going to end one way. It is apt really that the last game at Goodison Park is a game like this. Like an old school 80s game. There was not a load of quality in the game but it was wild, it had passion, it had fight. People wanted to antagonise each other and fight each other. It was fitting it ended in absolute chaos."

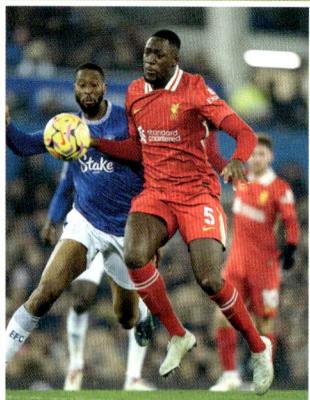

HEAD COACH:

ARNE SLOT

* Due to being sent off, Premier League rules prevented Arne Slot from commenting on this fixture.

CAPTAIN:

VIRGIL VAN DIJK

"I think conceding a goal in the last seconds of a game, or even after added time of a game, is very difficult. That hurt and should hurt for each one of us but it is the reality. You have two things you can do: you can dwell on it and stay angry about it or you can take it on board, start the recovery and be ready for the next game. We all know we could have played better, but we all know this is their game of the season and we've seen it over the years."

FOR THE RECORD:

This was the first time in Liverpool's top-flight history that the Reds named a starting XI with no English players in it.

ALSO THIS MIDWEEK:

No other matches

REPORT:

Goodison Park was never going to go quietly so it was somehow appropriate that the 120th and final Merseyside derby there ended in controversy and chaos.

Four goals, four red cards, fury and glory - it was an 'everybody on the dancefloor for a fight' kind of night with a slice of history at stake in addition to three points.

Liverpool crossed Stanley Park for Arne Slot's first derby day having won 41 and lost 41 of the previous 119 clashes at Goodison.

The memories came flooding back; Sandy Brown's own goal, Emlyn Hughes' double, Ian Rush hitting four, 4-4 in the FA Cup, Gary McAllister's 35-yard late winner, Steven Gerrard's smasher, Dirk Kuyt's double, Sadio Mane's Christmas cracker, Luis Suarez's diving celebration, Diogo Jota making it 4-1, but this was an opportunity for the victors to have eternal bragging rights for the most Goodison Park wins in the most-played top-flight derby.

It took a disputed stoppage-time equaliser to deny Liverpool that 42nd win, and coming on the back of the Reds' shock FA Cup exit at Plymouth it stung, but these Scouse squabbles have been littered with regret and recrimination in the previous 244 clashes so it was hardly a surprise.

Postponed 67 days earlier due to Storm Darragh, this was Liverpool's game in hand and an opportunity to go nine points clear at the top of the Premier League, but with Everton rejuvenated under the management of David Moyes and determined to have one last great night under the lights they started the better.

The first moment of controversy came in the 11th minute when Alexis Mac Allister was penalised for a foul on Iliman Ndiaye, despite making no contact with the Everton forward. From the free-kick, Beto ran into a space between Ibrahima Konate and Conor Bradley and slotted home with the Reds' appeals for offside in vain. 1-0 Everton, but not for long.

Five minutes later, Mac Allister won possession, found Konate and ran into the Blues' box to meet Mo Salah's cross with a glancing, looping header that beat the scrambling Jordan Pickford.

After Ndiaye went off injured a flurry of yellow cards followed with Andy Robertson, Jesper Lindstrom and Idrissa Gueye going into the book while Beto could have followed for an off-the-ball shove on Virgil van Dijk.

When Gueye pulled Cody Gakpo back in the 44th minute it looked a routine caution and two yellows equal red, but referee Michael Oliver kept his cards in his pocket much to the annoyance of the Liverpool bench.

Bradley was also booked before Dominik Szoboszlai forced Pickford into his first save of note in added-on time with James Tarkowski sliding in to deny Luis Diaz from the rebound.

Abdoulaye Doucoure wasted the best chance in the opening 10 minutes after the interval, heading Gueye's cross wide and with the Reds struggling to create anything Slot threw his Scouse duo, Trent Alexander-Arnold and Curtis Jones, into the fray.

Jarrad Branthwaite had a goal disallowed for offside against Jake O'Brien and by the 72nd minute Liverpool had failed to have a second-half shot, but Salah only needs one opportunity and in the 73rd minute he fired the Redmen ahead.

After a spell of possession Jones had a shot that Branthwaite blocked with his head, but he only directed the ball to Salah, who controlled it well and blasted home at the far post before running to the travelling Kop to celebrate.

It was his eighth Merseyside derby goal, only Gerrard (nine) has scored more and Salah almost equalled that tally in the 88th minute, but Pickford palmed his effort from the edge of the box over.

Five minutes of stoppage time were added on, but after a clash of heads that became eight and Everton snatched a dramatic, but controversial, equaliser when Tarkowski smashed the ball home at the far post after Konate was pushed in the back by Beto and Tim Iroegbunam flicked it on.

VAR official Chris Kavanagh checked for offside against Doucoure and a foul by Beto, but decided no offences were committed. In the 101st minute the goal was given and Evertonians celebrated like they'd won.

It all boiled over after the final whistle when Doucoure ran to the Liverpool fans to celebrate, prompting a furious reaction from Jones that sparked a melee. Both players were dismissed, as was Slot after saying something while shaking Michael Oliver's hand, with assistant manager Sipke Hulshoff also red carded.

Bramley Moore Dock has got some act to follow.

LIVERPOOL FC v WOLVERHAMPTON WANDERERS FC

REPORT:

With Arsenal having cut the Reds' lead at the top of the Premier League to four points, this was the one where Anfield got nervous.

Ahead of away trips to Aston Villa and Manchester City, it felt like a match that Liverpool needed to win. So when the Reds' creativity dried up and Wolves mounted a second-half comeback, Anfield got edgy.

The Reds had played three times since Vitor Pereira's men last kicked a ball 15 days earlier and while the visitors were fresher later in the game, Liverpool had the better of the first half on a bitterly cold Sunday afternoon.

A clever second-minute corner routine gave Trent Alexander-Arnold the first sight of goal, but he sliced his left-footed attempt wide. Diogo Jota also failed to connect with a left-footed volley as well as he'd hoped, sending it bouncing harmlessly past Jose Sa's post.

Wolves had lined up with wing-backs, but

were effectively playing a back five with a low block, making space at a premium. So when the Reds found a way through in the 15th minute it was something of an early relief.

Virgil van Dijk ended a Wolves attack with an immaculately-timed tackle in his own penalty area, Alexis Mac Allister moved the ball forward and Jota spun his man sublimely to send Luis Diaz charging down the left. He found Mo Salah with his cross, but when the Egyptian miscontrolled the ball Toti Gomes flicked out a leg and diverted it back towards Diaz.

The Colombian had continued his run into the box and bundled the ball past Sa with his midriff before being clattered on both shins by the Portuguese 'keeper. Had the ball not gone in a definite penalty and possible red card would have followed, but Liverpool led and that was quickly forgotten.

Jota would have made it 2-0 from Diaz's

LIVERPOOL FC 2
WOLVERHAMPTON WANDERERS FC 1

Goals: Diaz (15), Salah (37pen), Cunha (67)
16.02.25 · Anfield · Attendance: 60,401
Referee: Simon Hooper

LIVERPOOL (4-2-3-1): Alisson, Alexander-Arnold (Bradley 64), Konate (Quansah 46), Van Dijk (C), Robertson, Gravenberch, Mac Allister, Salah, Szoboszlai, Diaz (Endo 71), Jota (Nunez 64). Subs not used: Kelleher, Chiesa, Elliott, Tsimikas, McConnell. Booked: Konate, van Dijk.

WOLVES (3-4-2-1): Sa, Doherty, Agbadou (Bueno 61), T Gomes, Semedo (C) (Lima 90+2), Andre, J Gomes (Doyle 83), Ait-Nouri, Sarabia (Munetsi 46), Cunha, Guedes (Bellegarde 46). Subs not used: Bentley, Traore, Forbs, Djiga. Booked: Doherty, Peireira, Agbadou.

PRESS BOX:
PAUL JOYCE, THE TIMES

"The abiding snapshots of this match were of Liverpool resilience. Jarell Quansah slid in to deny the Wolves substitute Marshall Munetsi in the 88th minute, Virgil van Dijk celebrated blocking a Tommy Doyle free-kick and the ground rose to pay homage to Conor Bradley when he prevented Jean-Ricner Bellegarde from winning a corner. The substitute Wataru Endo brought another rousing cheer when he secured a foul from Pedro Lima just outside his own box that took precious seconds out of what had descended into a frenetic affair."

PUNDIT:
ASHLEY WILLIAMS, BBC MOTD 2

"Quansah found himself in a bit of a difficult position because Robertson had played Munetsi onside, but that is the type of defending you don't see that much any more – being out of position and having to sprint to make a [goal-saving] tackle. He goes with the opposite leg and that was as good as a goal for me."

HEAD COACH: ARNE SLOT

"At 2-0 up we had to deal with thinking we scored the 3-0, but completely the correct decision that he disallowed it for offside. Thinking we were going to score the 3-0 with a penalty [for] Mo, again, in my opinion, the correct decision for the VAR to turn that decision over. And then immediately receiving the 2-1, that is mentally not always easy – and that's why these wins are probably even more important than when we outplay Tottenham like we did here two weeks ago with 4-0. It's so difficult to win a game of football every three days after everything you go through in a season, so that's why this win is an important one going into a very tough week."

FOR THE RECORD:

This was the 17th consecutive game at Anfield in which the Reds have scored twice, surpassing the club record of 16 set in 1893/94.

ALSO THIS WEEKEND:

Leicester City 0-2 Arsenal
Manchester City 4-0 Newcastle United
Fulham 2-1 Nottingham Forest

cross had Emmanuel Agbadou not thrown himself in front of the ball to block, VAR checking he hadn't used his arm, and a commanding Van Dijk header created the next chance with Dominik Szoboszlai taking the loose ball on and sweeping a low shot across Sa's goal, but past the upright.

A mazy Ibrahima Konate run took him on a Joel Matip-esque adventure towards the Wolves box, but after losing possession he conceded a free-kick and was booked for kicking the ball away.

The Reds continued to press and when Sa pushed Andy Robertson's cross out to Jota he took a touch to evade a challenge before firing goalwards, but Sa was up to save with his feet. From the resulting corner Alexander-Arnold fired over from the edge of the box.

Diaz was a constant threat and when Mac Allister knocked a pass forward he nudged Agbadou to get to the ball first before touching it past Sa only to be brought down by the Wolves' keeper again. This time the ball didn't go in and referee Simon Hooper awarded a penalty.

Wolves howled for a foul by Diaz, but VAR didn't concur and Salah had the chance to make it 2-0. It was the 50th penalty he had taken for the Redmen and he clipped it straight down the middle after Sa dived to his left.

Konate could have received a second yellow card for barging into

Matheus Cunha, who curled the free-kick from the edge of the box narrowly wide, and he was replaced by Jarell Quansah at half-time.

Pereira also made a double substitution and a tactical tweak that changed the game to such an extent that Liverpool failed to have a single shot, on or off target, during the entire second half.

Never before had that happened in a Premier League match at Anfield and it turned into a test of resilience, a question of character. One the Reds just about passed.

Marshall Munetsi was just five minutes into his Premier League debut when he went clean through, but Alisson denied him with his face.

Salah scored again, but was offside just inside the Wolves half when beginning his run, and Jota was awarded a penalty following a challenge by Agbadou, but the referee overturned his decision after being sent to the pitch-side monitor for a review.

Cunha made Anfield anxious with a brilliant 67th-minute strike from over 20 yards. Then, in the 88th minute, Tommy Doyle's cross was about to be tapped in by Munetsi until Quansah slid in to make a challenge that was worth two points.

Liverpool had ground out a victory and Anfield breathed a sigh of relief.

ASTON VILLA FC 2
LIVERPOOL FC 2

Goals: Salah (29), Tielemans (38),
Watkins (45+3), Alexander-Arnold (61)

19.02.25 · Villa Park · Attendance: 41,910
Referee: Craig Pawson

ASTON VILLA (4-2-3-1): Martinez, Garcia (Cash 67), Disasi, Mings, Digne (Maatsen 78), McGinn (C) (Bogarde 86), Tielemans, Rogers, Asensio (Malen 67), Rashford (Ramsey 67), Watkins. Subs not used: Olsen, Zych, Jimoh-Aloba. Booked: Disasi, MacPhee.

LIVERPOOL (4-2-4): Alisson, Alexander-Arnold (Bradley 66, (Quansah 89)), Konate, Van Dijk (C), Robertson, Gravenberch, Mac Allister (Diaz 80), Salah, Szoboszlai, Jones, Jota (Nunez 66). Subs not used: Kelleher, Endo, Chiesa, Elliott, Tsimikas.

PRESS BOX:
IAN DOYLE, LIVERPOOL ECHO
"If the Premier League title was won by sheer desire, Mohamed Salah would have been declared a champion months ago. Rarely has one player clearly wanted to win the championship quite so much. To say Salah is on a mission would be something of an understatement. But that the Egyptian continues to back up his hunger with decisive actions underlines why he remains the one most likely responsible should Liverpool end the season with the 20th crown in the trophy cabinet."

PUNDIT:
ROBBIE FOWLER, TNT SPORTS
"It was a good point, eventually. Liverpool were losing the game 2-1 and got back into the game. It's a point gained. As a Liverpool fan, you want Liverpool to win the game and put in a performance. They worked hard and could have won the game, but so could Aston Villa in the end."

HEAD COACH:
ARNE SLOT
"What we must not do, and have done a bit too often now, is that we don't get what we deserve. If you look at all the chances, if you put them in a row from us and them, I think it's clear which team should have won this game. We must not make a habit out of that because it happened a bit too much now. Still, we are eight points clear of Arsenal."

FOR THE RECORD:
Mo Salah became the first Liverpool player to score 15 away goals in a Premier League season. Only Jimmy Smith (16 in 1929/30) has got more in a season.

ALSO THIS MIDWEEK:
No other matches

REPORT:
This was supposed to be Liverpool's first midweek off since New Year's Day, reward for avoiding the Champions League play-offs, but in football you can be victims of your own success.

Reaching the Carabao Cup final meant the Reds' trip to Villa Park, scheduled for the same weekend as Wembley, was brought forward by a month. And two days after this absorbing 2-2 draw, Arne Slot's side were drawn to face Paris Saint-Germain in the Champions League round of 16.

While the new format has breathed life into the competition, to 'reward' the inaugural league phase winners with a last 16 tie against the French champions, unbeaten in Ligue 1 all season and who won their play-off against Brest 10-0 on aggregate, suggests the format needs tweaking.

Aston Villa qualified automatically in eighth and drew Club Brugge, who'd finished 24th. Them's the breaks, but there isn't much incentive to finish top, unlike in the Premier League.

Slot was critical of his side's lack of clinical finishing after this game. The Reds had the chances to win, but missed too many, the only consolation being they continued their unbeaten run away from Anfield, a record matched only by PSG and Bayer Leverkusen in Europe's big leagues.

With Cody Gakpo missing due to an ankle injury and Luis Diaz rested after a hectic run of games, Slot adopted a 4-2-4 system with Curtis Jones and Dominik Szoboszlai operating centrally as false no9s.

Liverpool carved out the first opportunity from a short corner routine, Virgil van Dijk firing over at the far post, but it was Jota who had the best early chance. Alexis Mac Allister pressed John McGinn into giving Trent Alexander-Arnold the ball on the edge of the Villa box. He instantly picked out Jota, but he misdirected his header well wide.

Jota also shanked a volley past the post, much to the enjoyment of a Holte End who aren't fond of ex-Wolves players.

Marcus Rashford, making his first start since signing on loan from Manchester United, took similar stick from the travelling Kop after fouling Ibrahima Konate and thought he'd created the first goal when he got in behind the Reds' defence and his cross went in off Van Dijk, but he was offside.

Moments later, Jones showed nifty footwork to spin away from two Villa players and play a pass between the centre-backs for Szoboszlai to run onto, but Emi Martinez was off his line quickly to make the save.

Just before the half-hour mark, Liverpool made the breakthrough after a howler by Andres Garcia. Under pressure from Jones, he tried

to pass the ball back to Martinez, but only found Jota and he squared it for Salah to score.

Villa hit back eight minutes later when the Reds failed to clear a free-kick and Szoboszlai's header fell to Youri Tielemans, who rammed the ball home.

Almost immediately from the kick-off, Andy Robertson played Jota in but with just Martinez to beat he curled his shot well wide and that, plus a miss by Jones, looked costly in stoppage-time when Ollie Watkins headed a Lucas Digne cross past Alisson.

The Reds should have been out of sight, but somehow found themselves behind and it could've been 3-1 after the break when Rashford beat Alisson to a long ball, but Konate headed his chipped effort off the line.

Jota came even closer to scoring on the hour mark when he cut back inside after receiving a Ryan Gravenberch pass and struck the crossbar from 19 yards out. Just a minute later, the Reds were level.

Mac Allister won possession, Alexander-Arnold burst forward, exchanged passes with Salah and let fly from just inside the Villa box with a shot that clipped Tyrone Mings on its way over Martinez. 2-2, and it made Salah the first player to score and assist in 10 different games in a top-flight season since Barcelona's Lionel Messi in 2014/15. Which isn't bad company to keep.

Darwin Nunez and Conor Bradley came on and were immediately involved. Bradley's slide-rule pass played Szoboszlai in and he unselfishly squared it to Nunez, but the Uruguayan blazed over an open goal from six yards out.

It was Liverpool's 17th shot of the night, but only three were on target, and in the end Villa could have won it with Alisson saving from Donyell Malen, Jacob Ramsey having a goal disallowed for offside and Malen firing narrowly wide.

Rather than a midweek off for Liverpool, it was a midweek off target.

MANCHESTER CITY FC 0
LIVERPOOL FC 2

Goals: Salah (14), Szoboszlai (37)

23.02.25 · Etihad Stadium

Attendance: 52,803

Referee: Anthony Taylor

MAN CITY (4-2-4): Ederson, Lewis, Khushanov, Ake (Dias 77), Gvardiol, Savinho, Gonzalez (Kovacic 78), De Bruyne (C) (McAtee 66), Doku, Marmoush (Gundogan 77), Foden. Subs not used: Ortega, Grealish, Silva, Reis, Nunes.

LIVERPOOL (4-2-4): Alisson, Alexander-Arnold (Quansah 90+2), Konate, Van Dijk (C), Robertson (Tsimikas 74), Gravenberch, Mac Allister, Salah (Elliott 90+1), Szoboszlai, Jones (Endo 73), Diaz (Gakpo 79). Subs not used: Kelleher, Nunez, Chiesa, Jota.

PRESS BOX:
PAUL JOYCE, THE TIMES
"There was no more fitting venue than the home of the champions for Liverpool to deliver a statement performance that screamed of their intent to usurp them as England's finest. A coronation is surely coming. 'Hand it over, hand it over,' bellowed the away supporters in a stadium that had quickly emptied before following it up with the even more emphatic boast of 'We're gonna with the league'. This was ruthless versus toothless and by winning resoundingly at the Etihad for the first time in a decade, Arne Slot's side moved 11 points clear at the top."

PUNDIT:
DANIEL STURRIDGE, SKY SPORTS
"What Mohamed Salah is doing for Liverpool season in and season out is ridiculous, it's mindblowing. When he came to the club I don't think anyone thought that he would even be close to a guy that would score 25 goals a season or 20 goals a season. The consistency he has shown is incredible. If we are not linking him to the Ballon d'Or then it is getting out of hand. We have to start putting him in that conversation. He has not even been in the top three votes yet."

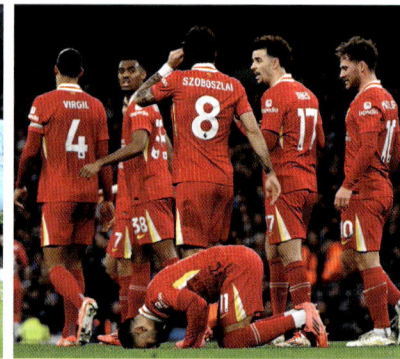

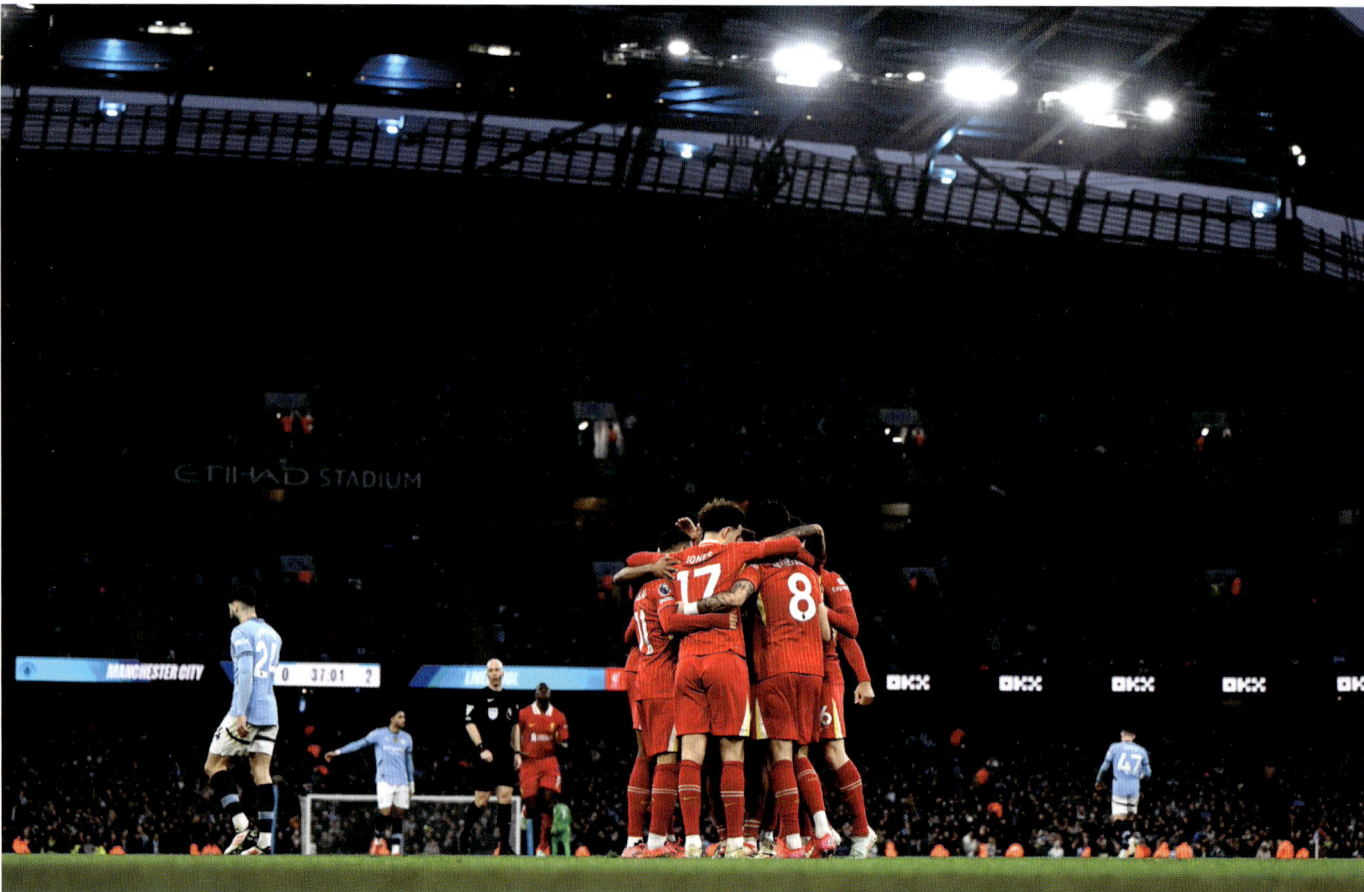

HEAD COACH:
ARNE SLOT

"If you play away at the Etihad, if you win there it is always a big win, no matter what the league table looks like. We had to defend a lot, we had to suffer a lot, they love ball possession. Especially in the second half I liked the way that we defended, even more so than in the first half, because in the first I felt constantly like they could score but we controlled it much better in the second. I am mostly happy because we won at the Etihad, and that is not something that happens a lot. It was my first time here but not many managers or teams win here, so we should be happy."

FOR THE RECORD:

Arne Slot became the second LFC manager to beat the reigning champions home and away in his first season in charge after Bob Paisley v Leeds United in 1974/75.

ALSO THIS WEEKEND:

Arsenal 0-1 West Ham United
Newcastle United 4-3 Nottingham Forest
Aston Villa 2-1 Chelsea

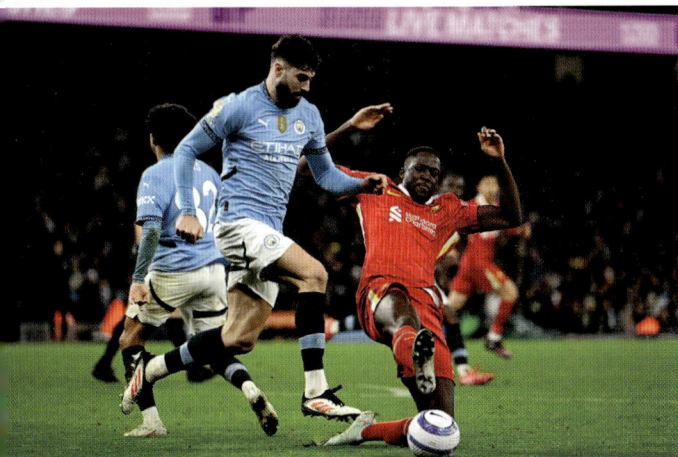

REPORT:

"Hand it over, hand it over, hand it over Manchester," bellowed the travelling Kop as Liverpool went 20 points clear of Manchester City to edge closer to a 20th league title.

The Reds hadn't won a Premier League game at the Etihad since 2016, but Arne Slot's first visit was much more than a 2-0 win and three points. It was a dethroning. A public toppling. The unseated Pep Guardiola might as well have placed a crown on Slot's head at full-time. Hand it over Manchester.

The Cityzens had won four titles in a row – only Liverpool's runaway victory in 2019/20 had prevented it from being seven on the bounce – but the sky blue ribbons could be packed away again. And with second-placed Arsenal having suffered a shock 1-0 home defeat to West Ham a day earlier, Liverpool ended the day with an 11-point lead with 11 games to play. As pivotal weekends in a title race go, this was massive.

Cody Gakpo was fit to return to the bench while City – knocked out of the Champions League by Real Madrid in midweek – were without Rodri and Erling Haaland among others. Just as he had at Aston Villa, Slot played Dominik Szoboszlai and Curtis Jones as false nines while Guardiola did something similar with Phil Foden and Omar Marmoush, although at times it was more like a 4-1-4-1.

Signed a month earlier, Marmoush had already scored a hat-trick in a 4-0 win against Newcastle, but it was the Egyptian in red who opened the scoring in the 14th minute.

Liverpool pressed City high up the pitch and Luis Diaz won a corner. Alexis Mac Allister struck it along the turf in the direction of Szoboszlai, who moved out of the six-yard box to run towards the ball. For a split-second it looked like Mac Allister had mis-hit it, but Liverpool development coach Aaron Briggs, who also devises set-pieces, had conjured up a new routine.

While still facing the corner flag, Szoboszlai sensationally clipped a no-look pass behind him to Mo Salah, who was completely unmarked close to the penalty spot. Salah let fly, the ball clipped Nathan Ake's shin and Ederson was beaten. 1-0, and Salah had his 30th goal of another prolific season.

City responded by stepping things up. Jeremy Doku got past Trent Alexander-Arnold a couple of times, but produced nothing with his final ball, while Marmoush tried a curler that Alisson easily gathered.

Salah's international teammate did find the net when played in by Foden on the half-hour mark, but was two yards offside. VAR didn't really need to look.

That was as close as the hosts came to actually scoring and with the Reds reasserting control they made it count.

Alexander-Arnold pinged a pass down the right that the offside Szoboszlai left for the onside Salah to run onto. He cut past Josko Gvardiol inside the City box and rolled the ball to Szoboszlai, who took a touch before wrong-footing Ederson with a low left-footed drive into the net. Jones had run into an offside position, but wasn't in the goalkeeper's eyeline. 2-0, and Salah had his 21st assist of another prolific season.

The sight of Ibrahima Konate celebrating a tackle like a goal a minute before half-time pumped the Liverpool supporters up even further and in the 57th minute they were celebrating again.

Szoboszlai raced onto Ryan Gravenberch's pass and squared for Jones to make it 3-0, but the dream stealers were lying in wait again in Manchester and VAR adjudged the Hungarian to be offside. That stay of execution perked City up and immediately from the restart Marmoush flashed a shot across goal.

Andy Robertson also fired an effort wide of goal before bursting forward on a counter-attack and finding Diaz, who cut inside and struck a shot that a full-stretch Ederson tipped onto the crossbar.

Savinho finally got in down the Liverpool left in the 75th minute, but Virgil van Dijk's intervention prevented Marmoush from tapping in before Rico Lewis hit the side-netting.

As the traditional Mancunian rain teemed down, Salah also forced Ederson to get down low to keep another shot out and when he played Szoboszlai in again it took a last-ditch sliding block by Abdukodir Khusanov to keep it at 2-0.

By the time Anthony Taylor blew his final whistle the Etihad was a sea of empty blue seats bar a bouncing patch of red, as they didn't want to hear it.

Hand it over, hand it over, hand it over Manchester.

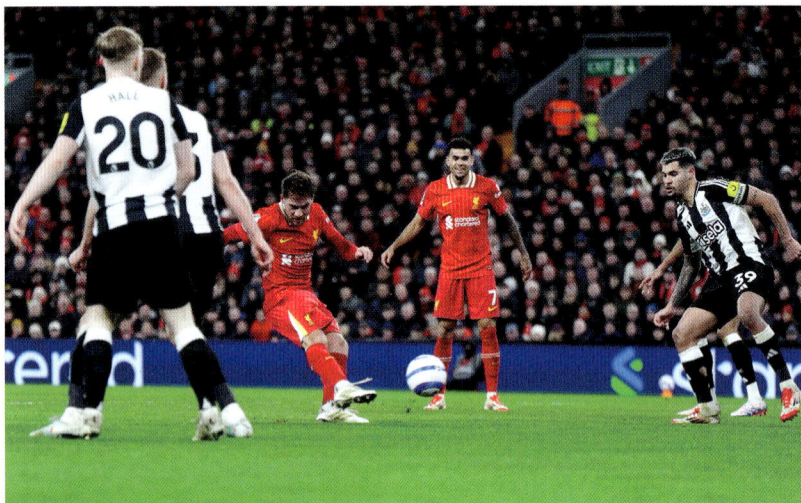

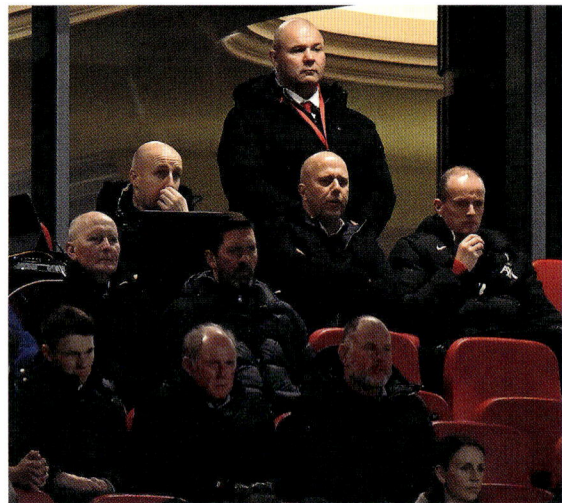

REPORT:

When Jürgen Klopp announced he was stepping down as Liverpool manager, nobody predicted that 13 months later a former Everton player would be on the Anfield touchline guiding the Reds to a 13-point lead at the top of the Premier League.

Yet that's precisely what happened as the Liver Bird saw off the Magpies by two goals to nil with John Heitinga standing in for the suspended Arne Slot. The Reds head coach watched from the back of the Directors' Box alongside assistant manager Sipke Hulshoff as the pair began the first of a two-game suspension for being sent off after the Merseyside derby at Goodison Park.

Fellow Dutchman Heitinga is no stranger to feisty derbies, having played in five Liverpool v Everton clashes, but leading the Redmen from the touchline was a new experience for the

assistant coach and one he passed with flying colours.

Liverpool bossed possession, reduced the Geordies to three shots on goal – none of which were on target – and took two of the 12 chances they created. With Alexander Isak missing with a groin injury, Newcastle were a damp squib on a wet Wednesday night that made Anfield's pitch slick and led to a surprisingly comfortable home win.

That was no bad thing, as it was Liverpool's fifth league match in 15 days and brought to an end a relentless run of games ahead of a rare weekend off, albeit due to the FA Cup exit at Plymouth, before PSG in the Champions League and a trip to Wembley for another date with Eddie Howe's side in the Carabao Cup final.

Kostas Tsimikas and Diogo Jota came back into the starting XI and referee Stuart Attwell had the home support up in arms early on

LIVERPOOL FC 2
NEWCASTLE UNITED FC 0
Goals: Szoboszlai (11), Mac Allister (63)
26.02.25 · Anfield · Attendance: 60,374
Referee: Stuart Attwell

LIVERPOOL (4-2-3-1): Alisson, Alexander-Arnold (Quansah 77), Konate, Van Dijk (C), Tsimikas, Gravenberch (Endo 77), Mac Allister (Jones 87) Salah, Szoboszlai, Diaz (Nunez 87), Jota (Gakpo 62). Subs not used: Kelleher, Chiesa, Elliott, Robertson.

NEWCASTLE (4-2-3-1): Pope, Livramento (Trippier 69), Schar, Burn, Hall, Guimaraes (C) (Longstaff 88), Tonali (Miley 69), Murphy, Gordon, Willock (Barnes 68), Wilson (Osula 69). Subs not used: Dubravka, Ruddy, Target, Krafth. Booked: Murphy.

PRESS BOX:
ANDY HUNTER, THE GUARDIAN
"At 9.22pm news filtered through of Arsenal's draw at Nottingham Forest in the earlier kick-off. The first chant of 'Liverpool, top of the league' emerged from the Kop.

Alexis Mac Allister soon added to Dominik Szoboszlai's first-half goal with an emphatic finish of his own and the title-winning atmosphere cranked up. Anfield was denied the chance to roar home league championship no19 due to the pandemic. The procession towards no20 affords Liverpool supporters plenty of time to make amends. The run-in is turning into a lap of honour."

PUNDIT:
DANNY MURPHY, BBC MATCH OF THE DAY
"It was classy, it was controlled, it was measured with some great performances, especially in midfield from Szoboszlai and Mac Allister. But I think Luis Diaz has gone under the radar a little bit. He's got a wonderful work ethic and attitude to the game wherever he is asked to play. A lot of the time this season he has been asked to play in the centre-forward role, but he was out wide because Jota played tonight. He was beating people, he was sharp and he loves running in behind without the ball.

He always does his defensive work and epitomises everything good about this Liverpool team and was a great replacement for Sadio Mane."

HEAD COACH: ARNE SLOT
"What impressed me most was that this was our fifth game in 15 days and the four before weren't the most simple ones. To show up the way we did tonight, hardly conceding a chance against a very good team like Newcastle, is a big compliment for the players in how they handled these five games in 15 days. Dominik deserves the credit he is getting at the moment. He already got my credit every single time he played for us, but probably he gets it now even more from the people who are judging players not only on work-rate but also goals and assists."

FOR THE RECORD:
This was the 29th consecutive home league game the Reds have scored in against Newcastle, a Premier League record, and made it 29 Anfield games undefeated against the Magpies.

ALSO THIS MIDWEEK:
Nottingham Forest 0-0 Arsenal
Tottenham Hotspur 0-1 Manchester City
Brighton & Hove Albion 2-1 Bournemouth

when Lewis Hall dragged Mo Salah down in the penalty area only for Newcastle to get the free-kick. Slot looked utterly baffled as he watched a replay in the Main Stand.

The next replay he saw was a Liverpool goal in the 11th minute. Alexis Mac Allister brought the ball forward and found Jota, who released Luis Diaz down the left. Pulled out of position, Fabian Schar backed off, and backed off and backed off until Diaz was so deep inside the Newcastle penalty area he could've shaken hands with Ant and Dec if they'd been on the front row of the away end.

He pulled the ball back and Dominik Szoboszlai struck a first-time shot with his left foot that nutmegged both Sandro Tonali and Dan Burn on its way past the outstretched arm of Nick Pope. It was the Reds' 50th Anfield goal of the season in their 20th game.

Mac Allister had a shot blocked and Tsimikas blazed another effort over before a long ball by Burn caught Ibrahima Konate out and sent Callum Wilson clear, but he bent the ball well wide of Alisson's far post. Wilson had also fluffed an earlier chance, later flagged for offside. Szoboszlai almost added a second when he clipped a shot just past the upright after Jota robbed Hall of possession and Salah curled over after Tsimikas bombed forward down the left on the counter-attack.

After a quiet start to the second period, Mac Allister took the game by the scruff of the neck to create and score Liverpool's second. After picking off a Tonali pass he brought the ball forward, slipped it to Salah and swept the return pass beyond Pope into the far corner.

It made it an 18th successive Anfield game in which the Reds had scored at least twice, a feat never before achieved under previous managers, and moments later chants of 'Liverpool, Liverpool, top of the league' filled the air when news filtered through that Arsenal had drawn at Nottingham Forest.

Alisson did well to push out Jacob Murphy's deflected cross to start a counter-attack that ended with Diaz sliding a splendid Salah cross – made with the outside of his boot – into the side-netting as Pope ended up in his own net.

Wataru Endo came on and bossed the midfield like a dad thrown into a kids' game and Salah also tried to score with his outstep from Szoboszlai's pass, but Pope got down to save. When Darwin Nunez won a corner his fellow sub Cody Gakpo bundled the ball home, but Konate was deemed to have fouled Pope and it remained 2-0.

Gakpo also sent an overhead-kick wide, but by then Heitinga's heroes had the game and a 13-point lead wrapped up.

LIVERPOOL FC 3
SOUTHAMPTON FC 1

Goals: Smallbone (45+1), Nunez (51), Salah (55pen), Salah (88pen)

08.03.25 · Anfield · Attendance: 60,399
Referee: Lewis Smith

LIVERPOOL (4-2-3-1): Alisson, Alexander-Arnold (Quansah 89), Konate, Van Dijk (C), Tsimikas (Robertson 46), Gravenberch (Endo 81), Jones (Mac Allister 46), Salah, Szoboszlai (Elliott 46), Diaz, Nunez (Jota 68). Subs not used: Kelleher, Chiesa, McConnell. Booked: Tsimikas, Nunez.

SOUTHAMPTON (4-2-3-1): Ramsdale, Walker-Peters, Bednarek (C) (Bella-Kotchap 19), Harwood-Bellis, Manning (Aribo 83), Ugochukwu (Onuachu 84), Smallbone (Lallana 71), Dibling (Sugawara 64), Fernandes, Sulemana, Gronbaek (Archer 64). Subs not used: McCarthy, Stephens, Wellington. Booked: Onuachu.

PRESS BOX:
LEWIS STEELE, DAILY MAIL
"The Liverpool attack was this week compared to 'three fighter jets' by Paris Saint-Germain boss Luis Enrique. But for 45 languid minutes against lowly Southampton, they resembled more of a run-of-the-mill budget plane with propellers, struggling to take flight. They were troubled by turbulence as the worst team in the league took a surprise lead and then they were given a rollicking by boss Arne Slot, watching on from the stands – air traffic control giving them a dressing-down if you want to stick with the analogy. Soon, Liverpool looked like the Red Arrows, zooming through the sky and leaving everything in their wake. Blink and you'll miss them."

PUNDIT:
RONNIE WHELAN, LFCTV
"Performances at this stage of the season are not really what you're looking for. You're looking to win games, and they did again. It wasn't pretty at times and they struggled first half, but then they controlled the second half.

They do that very well now, Liverpool, they control games until the end. They weren't particularly bothered about over-attacking, they just played the game as they saw it in front of them."

HEAD COACH: ARNE SLOT
"I said at half-time that energy levels were far, far, far too low. That is what had to change and that's why we made three substitutions just to, apart from bringing in quality, also create something. Because nine out of 10 times when you take three out, the other eight are like, 'Ooh, something else should happen'. That's the only thing I could come up with at half-time to create something different for the second half."

FOR THE RECORD:
This was Mo Salah's 250th victory for LFC in his 390th appearance, beating Ian Rush's club record of 250 wins in 416 games.

ALSO THIS WEEKEND:
Nottingham Forest 1-0 Manchester City
Manchester United 1-1 Arsenal
Brentford 0-1 Aston Villa

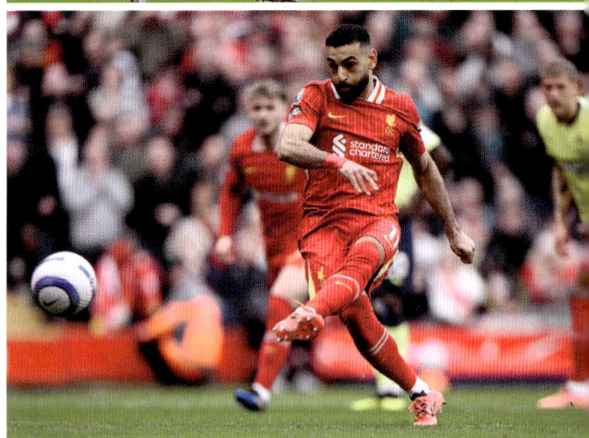

REPORT:
One of the reasons the Premier League is regarded as the best domestic division in the world is because of games like this.

Where else would a team top of the table, 58 points clear of their rock-bottom opponents, having won away at PSG in midweek, find themselves 1-0 down at half-time of a seemingly nailed-on home win?

Liverpool took nine points from their opening three games this season, the Saints turned up with nine points from 27 games. They also had their third different manager to face the Reds in four months and remained on course to beat Derby County's unwanted record low of 11 Premier League points, accumulated in a catastrophic 2007/08 campaign from which the Rams have never truly recovered.

Back then, Rafa Benitez's men thrashed Derby 6-0 at Anfield to go top of the league for the first time in four years, but almost two decades on the class of 2024/25 made such hard work of dispatching Southampton that Arne Slot – again watching from the Main Stand – made a triple half-time substitution.

There were mitigating circumstances. While Liverpool had beaten Paris Saint-Germain 1-0 in Parc des Princes in midweek, they had spent most of the night defending. Alisson had been busier than a Notre-Dame roof restorer, producing some sensational saves and keeping a clean sheet as PSG threw le kitchen sink at him before

Harvey Elliott's winner, but it was quickly evident against the Saints that it had been an energy-sapping night.

Curtis Jones squeezed an early shot just past the post and Trent Alexander-Arnold was denied by Aaron Ramsdale after a mazy Ryan Gravenberch dribble, but Liverpool were largely lethargic.

Jan Bednarek was forced off with a head injury in a concussion substitution, the rules meaning both sides could now make six changes, before Taylor Harwood-Bellis and Mateus Fernandes both gave Alisson work to do.

The Reds created a number of half-chances, Darwin Nunez hitting the best of them straight at Ramsdale, but inexplicably conceded a calamitous goal in first-half stoppage-time from a Ryan Manning throw-in. Virgil van Dijk tried to let the ball run through to Alisson, but Fernandes was behind him. He nicked the ball away from the Brazilian goalie for Will Smallbone to collect and he slotted it between Alisson's legs from a tight angle.

Slot was decisive in the dressing room. Kostas Tsimikas, Dominik Szoboszlai and Jones were all hooked, Andy Robertson, Alexis Mac Allister and Elliott were introduced. The idea was to give fresh impetus and energy. It worked a treat.

Elliott almost equalised in the 47th minute with a powerful cross-

shot that Ramsdale did well to divert past the post with his right wrist. Trent Alexander-Arnold and Robertson also tried their luck without success, but with the tempo massively upped, Southampton began to creak under the pressure and it was soon all-square.

Diaz ran at Kyle Walker-Peters like he was Stevie Heighway in his pomp and got to the byline before pulling the ball back for Nunez, who darted in front of the statuesque Armel Bella-Kotchap before opening the instep of his right-boot like it was a sand wedge to beautifully angle the ball past Ramsdale.

All of sudden the heady Anfield momentum that has sunk so many opponents over the years had Southampton in its clutches. Diaz twisted Walker-Peters inside out before forcing Ramsdale to parry his stinging drive and, from the rebound, Smallbone clumsily clattered into the back of Nunez's calves to send him tumbling.

Penalty, all day long, and although Ramsdale guessed the right way, Salah beautifully curled his penalty over the Saints' keeper to put the Reds ahead. Ivan Juric's side didn't throw in the towel and Cameron Archer stung Alisson's gloves after latching onto a Smallbone pass before Salah sliced a right-footed volley wide from a Diaz cross.

Salah's winner at St Mary's in November had come from the penalty spot following a handball by substitute Yukinari Sugawara and incredibly lightning struck twice for the Japanese international when, in an attempt to prevent Diaz running onto Andy Robertson's pass, he knocked the ball away with his elbow.

Referee Lewis Smith allowed play to continue, Diaz and Harwood-Bellis colliding as both slid in for the ball, but VAR official Matt Donohue had seen the handball and sent the official to the pitchside monitor.

Penalty, again, and for the third time this season Salah scored from the spot against Southampton to complete another comeback win, but Liverpool had to work for it.

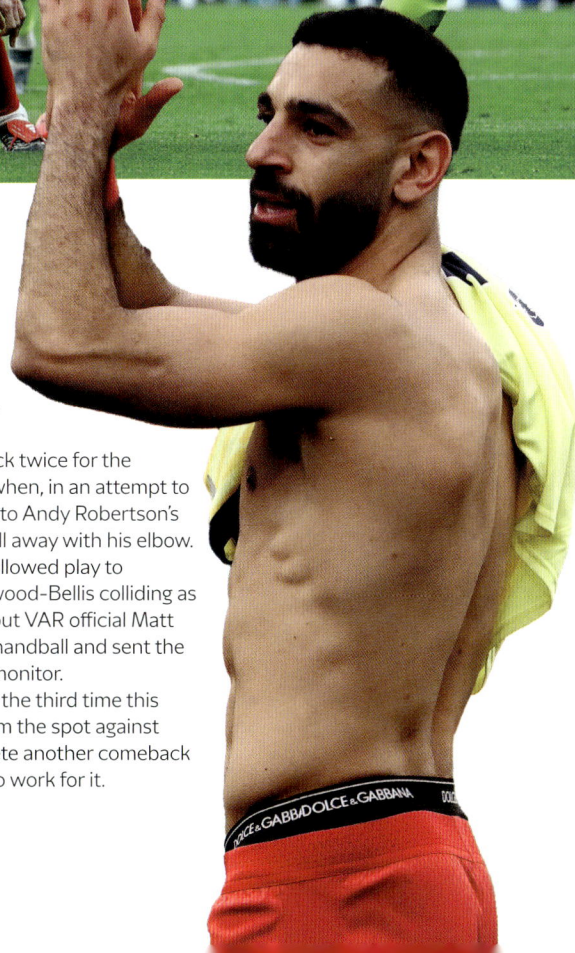

LIVERPOOL FC 1
EVERTON FC 0

Goal: Jota (57)

02.04.25 · Anfield

Attendance: 60,331

Referee: Sam Barrott

LIVERPOOL (4-2-3-1): Kelleher, Jones, Konate, Van Dijk (C), Robertson, Gravenberch, Mac Allister, Salah (Endo 90+3), Szoboszlai, Jota (Nunez 75), Diaz (Gakpo 86). Subs not used: Jaros, Chiesa, Elliott, Tsimikas, McConnell, Quansah. Booked: Jota, Nunez.

EVERTON (4-2-3-1): Pickford, O'Brien, Tarkowski (C), Branthwaite, Mykolenko, Garner (Iroegbunam 78), Gueye, Harrison (Ndiaye 69), Doucoure (Chermiti 86), Alcaraz (Young 78) Beto (Broja 79). Subs not used: Virginia, Patterson, Keane, Coleman. Booked: Tarkowski, Beto.

PRESS BOX:

ANDY DUNN, DAILY MIRROR

"In Grand National week on Merseyside, Diogo Jota made sure there will be no Devon Loch-style collapse in the title race. After their disappointments in the Champions League and Carabao Cup final, there were very faint suggestions that Arne Slot's side might falter dramatically in the Premier League run-in, but crossing the winning line is now a formality."

PUNDIT:

DUNCAN FERGUSON, SKY SPORTS

"There's no argument, straight red. Noticed it right away, how they never gave the decision...it's a straight red. Back in our day you might have got away with that because you've tackled, you've got the ball, but he [Tarkowski] knows what he's doing, he's come right through him. That could have been a leg-breaker, straight red all game long."

LIVERPOOL FC v EVERTON FC

HEAD COACH:
ARNE SLOT

"At Goodison Park we had ball possession, but we only had ball possession with our centre-backs and full-backs. I think if I say 10 or 15 times that Lucho Diaz was one-v-one against Jake O'Brien today, I don't even think I exaggerate, but to have that is one thing and to create a chance is another thing. That's why we have to be there so many times, so many times, so many times and you're hoping that one time can then be enough – and it was with Diogo's goal."

FOR THE RECORD:

The attendance of 60,331 was the highest ever for a Merseyside derby at Anfield while the 49-day gap between league derbies was the shortest since 1968 (42 days).

ALSO THIS MIDWEEK:

Arsenal 2-1 Fulham
Nottingham Forest 1-0 Manchester United
Bournemouth 1-2 Ipswich Town

REPORT:

Perceptions are powerful in football, even when they're not always true. Liverpool headed into the 246th Merseyside derby having been knocked out of the Champions League on penalties by PSG, following a 1-0 Anfield defeat, and beaten 2-1 at Wembley by Newcastle United in the Carabao Cup final, Federico Chiesa getting a late goal.

All of a sudden the talk was that Liverpool needed a win. That the wheels were falling off. That their form had nosedived. That if they didn't beat Everton at Anfield it would allow Arsenal to come careering over the hill and snatch the Premier League trophy out of Virgil van Dijk's hands. The reality was somewhat different.

Liverpool had saved their worst display of the season for Wembley, but came into the derby on the back of seven wins and two draws in their previous nine Premier League games. If taking 23 points from a possible 27 to lead the table by 12 points makes your next game 'need to win', then the other 19 clubs must have been in some trouble, but the Reds doused all the nonsense – some of it aimed at trying to keep the title-race going – by making Liverpool v Everton a did-win game.

The Blues crossed Stanley Park for the final time, unless they take a detour from the Hill Dickinson Stadium next season, unbeaten in nine and with manager David Moyes trying to win at Anfield for the first time in his 22nd attempt.

Liverpool knew victory would be their 100th against Everton and had Caoimhin Kelleher back in goal, Alisson ruled out after suffering a concussion on international duty with Brazil, while Curtis Jones played at right-back with both Trent Alexander-Arnold and Conor Bradley sidelined. Kopites also unfurled a huge 'We Made This City' banner in response to Everton's 'We Built This City' flag on display at Goodison Park 49 days earlier. A red card should also have been on display in the 11th minute.

After Diogo Jota had a shot blocked, Alexis Mac Allister won possession but was taken out by a thumping 'ball-and-all' challenge from Blues skipper James Tarkowski, his follow-through catching the Argentine on the back of his calf, causing his ankle to bend beneath him. Referee Sam Barrott brandished a yellow card, but when the replays showed how out of control the tackle was a red seemed inevitable, yet VAR official Paul Tierney failed to recommend a dismissal. When even Duncan Ferguson is calling it 'a leg-breaker', you know they've got it badly wrong.

Thankfully, Mac Allister was okay to continue, but Dominik Szoboszlai curled the free-kick wide. Perhaps the incident shook the Reds a little as Everton subsequently got into the game and Beto had a goal disallowed for offside after running onto a long ball from Tarkowski. Jota flashed a shot across goal and Mo Salah headed a Luis Diaz cross straight at Jordan Pickford before Beto had the best chance of all when he got away from Van Dijk to race clean through and shoot beyond Kelleher, but hit the post.

Liverpool shifted up a gear after the interval and had a flurry of chances. Pickford pushed Gravenberch's shot out before Mac Allister, Jota and Diaz had efforts blocked. The pressure was mounting and in the 57th minute came the decisive moment.

Jota tackled James Garner on the edge of the Everton box, Diaz backheeled the ball into his path and Jota slalomed past three Blues defenders like they were flags on the slopes of Lillehammer before slotting the ball back across Pickford into the Kop net.

Everton wanted an offside against Diaz, but he was off in a previous phase of play when he didn't attempt to get the ball. The goal stood and the 'Oh he wears the number 20' Jota song rang around Anfield louder than it has ever done before.

Chances were few and far between afterwards. Jarrad Branthwaite glanced Andy Robertson's cross past his own post and Diaz had a shot blocked by Tarkowski inside the six-yard box before a curious incident saw Pickford fly out and clatter Darwin Nunez above the knee, after play had been stopped for a foul on Szoboszlai, but it was the Uruguayan who was booked after receiving treatment.

Wataru Endo replaced Salah, signalling Slot was ready to take the 1-0 by sending his enforcer on, and when the final whistle blew it both sparked celebrations amongst a crowd that included Steven Gerrard and shifted skewed perceptions back to reality.

Liverpool are gonna win the league.

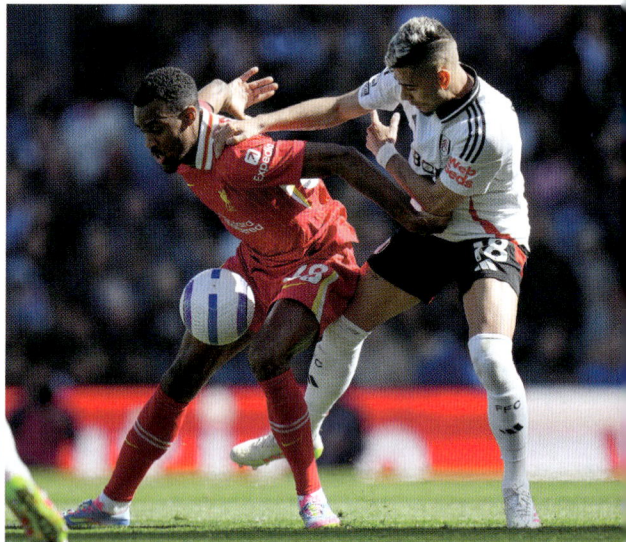

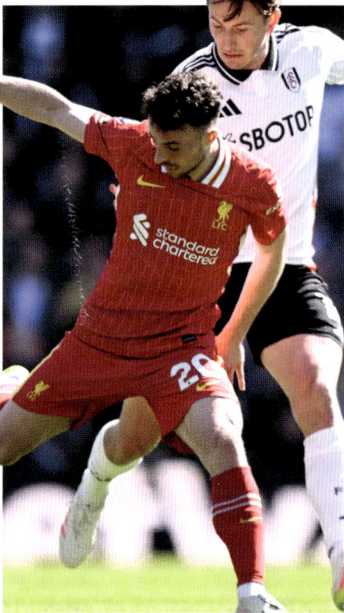

REPORT:

Of all the things Liverpool have achieved over the years, going unbeaten away from Anfield in a top-flight league season isn't one of them.

Even in the Reds' previous 19 title-winning campaigns they have lost at least once on their travels, so to arrive at Craven Cottage undefeated in all 15 of Arne Slot's league games away from Anfield was testament to their consistency over the last eight months.

However, any hopes of becoming just the fourth club – after Preston North End (1888/89), Arsenal (2001/02 and 2003/04) and Man United (2020/21) – to be invincible away from home were ended by a surprisingly error-prone first half defensive collapse at Fulham that saw three goals shipped in 13 minutes.

An uncharacteristic number of mistakes undid Liverpool, not in keeping with the Slot era so far, but then history shows that the Reds' title-winning teams tend to throw in a performance like this along the way.

Back in 2019/20, Jürgen Klopp's mentality monsters took 79 points from a possible 81 in their opening 27 matches and then inexplicably lost 3-0 at Watford, who ended the season relegated.

In 1989/90, King Kenny Dalglish's champions were thrashed 4-1 at Southampton, while Joe Fagan's 1983/84 treble-winners were on the end of a 4-0 thumping at Coventry City. Even Bob Paisley's class of 1978/79, who only conceded 16 goals in 42 games, lost 3-1 at mid-table Aston Villa having let in just two goals in their previous 13 matches.

So while this 3-2 reverse to end Liverpool's 26-game unbeaten run was untimely in terms of the title race, it wasn't without precedent and the fact that none of the top five won this weekend meant the damage was minimal.

Ibrahima Konaté's fifth-minute mistake set the tone. Trying to turn away from Andreas Pereira in his own box he was tackled and as Caoimhin

FULHAM FC 3
LIVERPOOL FC 2

Goals: Mac Allister (14), Sessegnon (23), Iwobi (32), Muniz (37), Diaz (72)
06.04.25 · Craven Cottage · Attendance: 27,770
Referee: Chris Kavanagh

FULHAM (4-2-3-1): Leno, Castagne, Andersen, Bassey, Robinson (C), Berge, Lukic (Reed 76), Sessegnon (Traore 82), Pereira (Smith-Rowe 76), Iwobi (Tete 82), Muniz (Jimenez 76). Subs not used: Benda, Cairney, Cuenca, Willian. Booked: Lukic, Smith-Rowe, Leno.

LIVERPOOL (4-2-3-1): Kelleher, Jones, Konate (Bradley 67), Van Dijk (C), Robertson (Chiesa 82), Gravenberch, Mac Allister, Salah, Szoboszlai (Elliott 55), Gakpo (Diaz 55), Jota (Nunez 67). Subs not used: Jaros, Endo, Tsimikas, Quansah.

PRESS BOX:
KIERAN JACKSON, THE INDEPENDENT
"Who saw this coming? The 27,000 at Craven Cottage certainly didn't, such was the state of utter stupefaction in the stands on a spring afternoon to remember in south-west London. Fulham were both dazzling and dogged and, indisputably, deserved winners. For Premier League champions-in-waiting Liverpool, though, it was simply a day to forget. One to write off. By extension for their defence, the opening period saw an utter implosion from all corners."

PUNDIT:
SHAY GIVEN, BBC MATCH OF THE DAY 2
"Fulham were brilliant going forward and Liverpool were very poor defensively. They had 15 minutes of madness in the first half and it's not like Liverpool at all. We've seen them defend so well and they're top of the league for a reason – because they're brilliant at the back. Curtis Jones was playing out of position – we know he's not a right-back, he's fitting in for Trent, but Conor Bradley was back on the bench today and he came on for the second half. Mentally they weren't tuned in for the first half."

HEAD COACH:
ARNE SLOT
"There is no reason for us to be complacent. We are not number one at the moment because we win every game with a margin of three or four goals. I think everyone who has seen our games [knows] it takes us so much effort, so much hard work to win games of football, combined with quality of course. We are fully aware of the fact we have to compete for seven more games. We saw it on Wednesday when we played Everton, it was a close call. Today it was a close call and many times we've been on the right side. Today we were on the wrong side, mainly because of the errors we made."

FOR THE RECORD:
Luis Diaz's goal was Liverpool's 35th at Craven Cottage in the Premier League, one more than the Reds have scored against Fulham at Anfield (34).

ALSO THIS WEEKEND:
Everton 1-1 Arsenal
Manchester United 0-0 Manchester City
Aston Villa 2-1 Nottingham Forest

Kelleher tried to prevent the Fulham man from squaring it to Rodrigo Muniz, he swept him off his feet. Play continued, Ryan Sessegnon shot wide and VAR surprisingly didn't intervene.

That was a huge let-off and the Reds made the most of it in the 14th minute when Ryan Gravenberch won possessions and Alexis Mac Allister brought the ball forward between two Fulham players before unleashing a shot from 25 yards that flew over Bernd Leno. Belter.

Having won 19 of the 20 Premier League games they'd scored first in, you wouldn't have found too many people predicting a Liverpool loss, but then came a 13-minute capitulation.

It started when Curtis Jones, again deputising at right-back, inadvertently diverted a cross to the far post back across goal for Sessegnon to slam the ball home.

Andy Robertson was next to catch erroritis when he tried to switch play with a diagonal ball, but only picked out Alex Iwobi on the edge of the Liverpool box. Gravenberch blocked his original effort, but Robertson had sprinted across trying to make up for his initial mistake and knocked the ball back to Iwobi before deflecting the Fulham forward's drive over Kelleher.

Virgil van Dijk was next to have regrets when he failed to deal with an Iwobi up and under that Muniz brought down brilliantly before

nutmegging Kelleher with his finish. For once, the travelling Kop were left stunned.

Liverpool should have reduced the deficit early in the second period after Mo Salah tackled Calvin Bassey and sent Diogo Jota through between two Cottagers defenders, but Leno flicked out a hand to nudge his shot inches past the post.

It wasn't only Liverpool's back four who were making unusual mistakes as when Luis Diaz crossed in the 64th minute, Salah arrived unmarked at the far post, seven yards out. Most days it's a goal, but he sent a half-volley high into the Putney End, much to the surprise of everyone, including himself.

Conor Bradley was introduced for Konate, Gravenberch moving to centre-back, and his energy livened the Reds up. Bradley had been on for five minutes when he burst forward and slipped a pass inside for Diaz, who showed quick feet to take a touch and score. Game on.

Harvey Elliott had an attempt saved and in the 79th minute the ex-Fulham man came even closer to equalising with a curling shot that beat Leno, but rattled the crossbar.

Kelleher prevented Harrison Reed from making it 4-2, but when Leno saved stoppage-time shots from Federcio Chiesa and Elliott, Liverpool's unbeaten away run was over. It was one of those days.

LIVERPOOL FC 2
WEST HAM UNITED FC 1

Goals: Diaz (18), Robertson (86og), Van Dijk (89)

13.04.25 · Anfield · Attendance: 60,376

Referee: Andy Madley

LIVERPOOL (4-2-3-1): Alisson, Bradley (Quansah 68), Konate, Van Dijk (C), Tsimikas (Robertson 60), Gravenberch, Mac Allister, Salah (Endo 85), Jones (Szoboszlai 68), Diaz, Jota (Gakpo 60). Subs not used: Jaros, Kelleher, Chiesa, Elliott.

WEST HAM UNITED (3-4-2-1): Areola, Todibo (Guilherme 78), Mavropanos, Kilman, Wan-Bissaka, Soler (Fullkrug 78), Ward-Prowse, Scarles (Coufal 57), Kudus, Paqueta, Bowen (C). Subs not used: Fabianski, Alvarez, Rodriguez, Soucek, Emerson, Ferguson. Booked: Coufal, Paqueta.

PRESS BOX:
IAN LADYMAN, DAILY MAIL
"It was captain Virgil van Dijk who rescued his team, though a sudden rediscovery of communal urgency and energy was just as much to thank. It's funny how it goes like that. Liverpool had been absent as an attacking force for half an hour, sucked back towards their own goal by doubt and uncertainty and maybe even some fear. But desperation enlivened them. Sport and psychology wrapped up together once more."

PUNDIT:
RAY HOUGHTON, LFCTV
"One thing Liverpool have had all season is goals in the team, that never-say-die attitude. In the last 10-15 minutes it looked more likely that West Ham were going to get a winner than Liverpool the way the game was going, but I thought they really upped it, Liverpool, and got after West Ham and got their opportunity which led to the goal. It was pure relief in the stadium, everyone

REPORT:
Sometimes you just need your skipper to deliver.

Liverpool went into this Anfield clash against West Ham United on a high. Mo Salah had signed a new contract and second-placed Arsenal had dropped points at home to Brentford, but just when it looked like a late own goal was going to mean the Reds failed to capitalise, Virgil van Dijk rose to the occasion in his 100th league game in the armband.

Our centre-half, our number four, lifted his first trophy as Liverpool captain after scoring the winner himself, Chelsea defeated in extra-time of the 2024 Carabao Cup final at Wembley. That was a farewell present to Jürgen Klopp, but when the towering Dutchman delivered another crucial winner here in the 89th minute, it edged Arne Slot ever closer to giving Liverpudlians the ultimate welcome gift.

Virgil had been involved in the Hammers' 86th-minute equaliser,

his attempted clearance ricocheting into the net off Andy Robertson, who was so annoyed they could probably hear him shout 'Virg' back in Glasgow, but just when the Redmen were wilting and West Ham flourishing, Van Dijk headed home an Alexis Mac Allister corner to almost blow the roof off the Kop.

That Liverpool needed such a late intervention was surprising given their first-half dominance. After the 97 were remembered with a Kop mosaic and period of silence two days before the 36th anniversary of the Hillsborough disaster, the Reds spent the opening 45 minutes in control.

Luis Diaz had a shot saved, Mac Allister headed over, Conor Bradley saw an effort deflected wide and Salah put one the wrong side of Alphonse Areola's post.

was like 'thank goodness for that'. It's three points closer to the end game and the end game is winning the Premier League."

HEAD COACH: ARNE SLOT

"I think the first 32 games have shown us how difficult it is – not only for us but for every team in the Premier League – to win a game of football. So the competition has never been as strong as it is this season. West Ham are 16th or 17th in the league but I can name you one or two players that could have easily played with us today in terms of quality. That is what the Premier League is about."

FOR THE RECORD:

This was Liverpool's 14th win in the 14 games Virgil van Dijk has scored in at Anfield, surpassing Alec Lindsay's club record of 13.

ALSO THIS WEEKEND:

Arsenal 1-1 Brentford
Newcastle United 4-1 Manchester United
Chelsea 2-2 Ipswich Town

The Hammers had 19-year-old Oliver Scarles at left wing-back and Salah gave him a torrid time, culminating in Liverpool's 18th-minute opener. Ibrahima Konate chipped a pass down the line and Salah tempted Scarles into trying to win it before using his body to expertly spin away from him.

Mo Salah, Mo Salah, was running down the wing and with the outside of his left boot he prodded a pass across goal for the unmarked Diaz to sweep home at the far post. If it was on an app for good-looking goals, you'd swipe right.

Diaz acknowledged Salah's James-inspired Kop song by sitting down next to him to celebrate on the electronic advertising boards, but moments later Alisson had to arch his back to somehow fingertip a Mohammed Kudus chip onto the crossbar after the Liverpool

'keeper had initially denied Carlos Soler. Salah continued to probe the Hammers' defence and created the next chance with a laser-like pass for the forward-running Mac Allister to meet on the volley, but Areola palmed his shot away.

Alisson made another top-class stop from Kudus, who was a yard offside anyway, before Konstantinos Mavropanos had a gilt-edge opportunity to equalise when he steamed in to meet a James Ward-Prowse corner seven yards out, but headed the ball into row two of the Kop.

Two minutes after the teams re-emerged, Kostas Tsimikas was tripped on the edge of the box and Mac Allister curled the free-kick goalwards, but it had a date with the crossbar. When a corner was cleared back to him, Mac Allister also sent a shot spinning towards goal that Areola had to acrobatically turn over.

Hammers boss Graham Potter substituted Scarles and switched to a back four shortly afterwards and it transformed his team. Jarrod Bowen evaded the offside trap to latch onto Lucas Paqueta's through-ball, but Alisson raced out to block.

Alisson also got down low to paw out a cross-shot from the dangerous Kudus, but the warning signs were flashing and Liverpool cracked. Aaron Wan-Bissaka got in behind Jarrell Quansah, on for Bradley, and sent in a low cross that Van Dijk struck against Robertson for an avoidable oggy.

Liverpool woke up again and Diaz almost restored the Reds' lead when he fired a Quansah pass goalwards only for Wan-Bissaka to deflect it against the bar.

Quansah also had a header blocked, after Diaz recycled Mac Allister's corner, before the Argentine tackled Paqueta and forced Areola to save at his near post.

The Hammers appealed for a foul, but Mac Allister sent in an outswinger and Van Dijk arrived like a cruise liner sailing up the River Mersey to score with a downward header. Boom.

Niclas Fullkrug almost killed the vibe when he headed against the crossbar in the 94th minute, but sometimes you just need your skipper to deliver and Virgil van Dijk marked a century in the armband with a captain's knock.

LEICESTER CITY FC 0
LIVERPOOL FC 1

Goal: Alexander-Arnold (76)
20.04.25 · King Power Stadium
Attendance: 30,402
Referee: Stuart Attwell

LEICESTER (4-2-3-1): Hermansen, Pereira (Justin 83), Faes, Coady, Thomas, Ndidi (Skipp 83), Soumare, De Cordova-Reid (Buonanotte 61), El Khannouss, Mavididi (Monga 85), Vardy (C) (Daka 62). Subs not used: Stolarczyk, Okoli, Kristiansen, Ayew. Booked: Ndidi.

LIVERPOOL (4-2-3-1): Alisson, Bradley (Alexander-Arnold 71), Konate, Van Dijk (C), Tsimikas, Gravenberch, Mac Allister, Salah, Szoboszlai (Elliott 71), Gakpo (Jota 60), Diaz (Jones 90+4). Subs not used: Kelleher, Endo, Nunez, Robertson, Quansah. Booked: Alexander-Arnold.

PRESS BOX:
JASON BURT, DAILY TELEGRAPH
"It had to be him. It just had to be. 'The Scouser in our team,' sang the jubilant Liverpool fans after Alexander-Arnold ran to them and, bare-chested, placed that number 66 shirt on a corner flag. The full-back had only been on the pitch for five minutes, having replaced Conor Bradley. All eyes now on Arsenal at home to Crystal Palace on Wednesday. If they lose then Liverpool will have claimed a 20th league title and Alexander-Arnold will have made the decisive intervention."

PUNDIT:
JAMIE CARRAGHER, SKY SPORTS
"Liverpool were in better form in the winter months, but they are getting the job done. Watching this game, you come away thinking it could be a bit more spectacular, but then you look at the amount of shots and big chances they created. Liverpool have scored 75 goals in the Premier League this season, which is brilliant, and I still feel they can score more goals."

HEAD COACH:
ARNE SLOT
"I think we created two very big chances in the first five minutes, in the first 15-20 minutes of the second half we created chance after chance, in my opinion. Since I've been here I don't think we played a game where we've had so many big chances and didn't score one of them. In the end we needed a set-piece to score, which wasn't a big chance, but a great finish from Trent. It was a big moment for us to score from a set-piece with us putting so much effort in for nine or 10 months now. It feels really good that in the moment we needed it most we scored from a set-piece."

FOR THE RECORD:
Trent Alexander-Arnold's goal was his first for Liverpool with his left foot and meant the Reds continued their run of scoring in every away league match this season.

ALSO THIS WEEKEND:
Ipswich Town 0-4 Arsenal
Aston Villa 4-1 Newcastle United
Manchester United 0-1 Wolves

REPORT:
When Trent Alexander-Arnold scored in Liverpool's 4-0 win at Leicester en route to winning the Premier League in 2019/20, it was first v second on a chilly Boxing Day.

Half-a-decade later, his dramatic Easter Sunday winner at the King Power Stadium sent the Foxes to the Championship as the Reds hopped three points closer to the title.

Arsenal's win at Ipswich earlier in the day meant Liverpool couldn't become champs at the stadium where they won the FA Community Shield in 2022. It also meant Man United were mathematically safe from relegation, despite losing at home to Wolves.

The travelling Kop were in a boisterous mood, proclaiming 'we're gonna win the league' in the East Midlands sunshine within moments of kick-off and they almost had a third-minute goal to celebrate.

A line of six defenders across the edge of the box didn't stop a simple Luis Diaz pass from picking Leicester open and Mo Salah calmly slotted past Mads Hermansen only for the ball to strike the inside of both posts before coming back out and being cleared. Salah rubbed his head in disbelief, like he'd seen an optical illusion.

Leicester, champions in 2016, were trying to avoid the unwanted record of becoming the first Premier League team to fail to score in nine consecutive home matches and came mightily close to taking a 10th-minute lead.

Stephy Mavididi showed Conor Bradley a clean pair of heels before cutting inside and sliding a pass to Wilfred Ndidi, who struck a low shot against Alisson's upright. From the rebound, Liverpool counter-attacked at pace. Diaz released Cody Gakpo and his cross was met on the volley by Salah, but Hermansen pushed the shot away.

As Liverpool supporters continued to go through the Anfield Songbook, Arne Slot's lads continued to press and another Salah volley, from a Kostas Tsimikas cross, was deflected behind by Luke Thomas.

Hermansen also saved Gakpo's diving-header, after Diaz lofted the ball across goal, while the Foxes' goalie also had to claw away a curler from the Dutch international with Salah closing in. From the corner, Ibrahima Konate angled a header goalwards, but this time Ndidi cleared from a couple of yards out with Salah ready to tap in.

Still the Reds advanced, still the Reds couldn't score. Gakpo shot straight at Hermansen, Salah lifted a powerful Tsimikas cross over and Diaz chested down Dominik Szoboszlai's flick, did a keep-up and shot on the turn, but wide of the target. It was Liverpool's 14th failed attempt of the first half and they began the second stanza with more urgency.

Szoboszlai's long-range drive was parried by Hermansen and just before Gakpo pounced on the rebound Conor Coady, formerly of this parish, nicked the ball away.

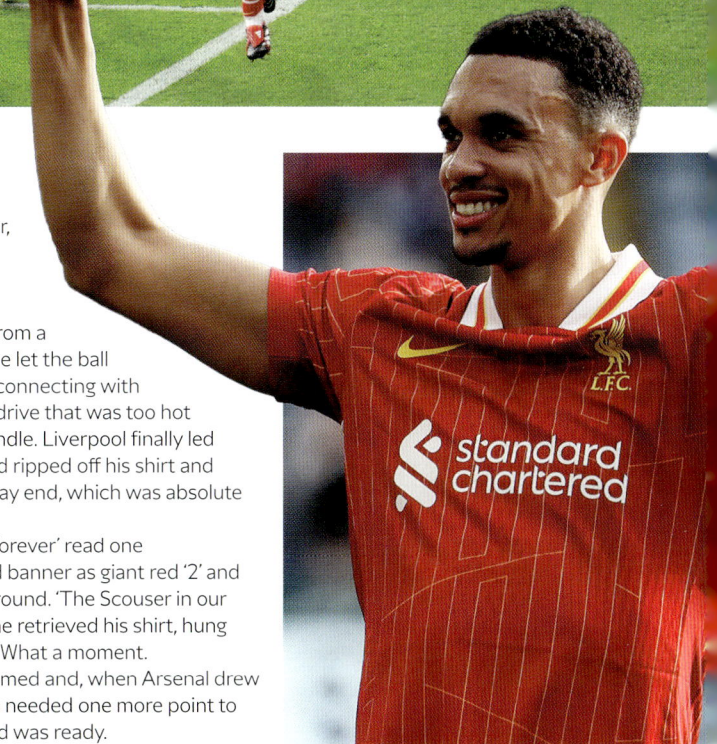

Slick combination play between Bradley, Salah and Ryan Gravenberch down the right ended with Diaz volleying Bradley's cross narrowly over. Diaz was in the thick of it and after he somehow won a 3v1 battle against Ndidi, Wout Faes and Ricardo Pereira the ball ran to Tsimikas, but Hermansen denied him that elusive first LFC goal.

Salah bent a shot past the post after more good work by the impressive Bradley and Diogo Jota, on for Gakpo, headed an opportunity wide. Maybe it wasn't our day.

There was a scare at the other end when, from a half-cleared free-kick, Coady headed home, but Patson Daka had barged Alisson out of the way before lifting the ball back across goal and it was disallowed.

Slot introduced Alexander-Arnold, for his return from injury, and Harvey Elliott and the pair combined to force a 76th-minute corner. Tsimikas curled the ball in, Virgil van Dijk – fresh from signing a new contract – flicked on and Salah headed against the post. The ball rebounded to Jota, who hit the bar, before Boubakary Soumare tried to clear, but headed the ball towards Alexander-Arnold.

Twelve yards out, from a slightly acute angle, he let the ball bounce once before connecting with a sizzling left-footed drive that was too hot for Hermansen to handle. Liverpool finally led and Alexander-Arnold ripped off his shirt and ran to the jubilant away end, which was absolute bedlam.

'It's Not Nineteen Forever' read one Courteeners-inspired banner as giant red '2' and '0' balloons floated around. 'The Scouser in our team' rang out after he retrieved his shirt, hung upon the corner flag. What a moment.

Leicester were doomed and, when Arsenal drew in midweek, the Reds needed one more point to be champions. Anfield was ready.

LIVERPOOL FC 5
TOTTENHAM HOTSPUR FC 1

Goals: Solanke (12), Diaz (16), Mac Allister (24), Gakpo (34), Salah (63), Udogie (69og)

27.04.25 · Anfield · Attendance: 60,415
Referee: Tom Bramall

LIVERPOOL (4-2-3-1): Alisson, Alexander-Arnold (Endo 76), Konate, Van Dijk (C), Robertson, Gravenberch, Mac Allister (Nunez 83), Salah, Szoboszlai (Jones 68), Diaz (Elliott 76), Gakpo (Jota 68).
Subs not used: Kelleher, Chiesa, Tsimikas, Quansah. Booked: Gakpo, Elliott.

TOTTENHAM (4-3-3): Vicario, Spence, Danso, Davies, Bergvall, Udogie, Gray (Sarr 46), Maddison (C) (Kulusevski 46), Johnson, Solanke (Richarlison 67), Tel (Odobert 68). Subs not used: Kinsky, Bissouma, Romero, Porro, Van de Ven. Booked: Richarlison.

REPORT:

Anfield was a sea of red, just like Virgil van Dijk had requested. "Come in red or come with all red," said the skipper after signing his new contract. "Make it a red Anfield because that would look incredible."

He was right. It looked a picture for Liverpool FC's title-winning day. Outside, rivers of red flowed round the streets of Anfield Road. Today was the day.

An estimated 120,000 LFC supporters were reportedly in the Anfield vicinity. Arne Slot's men still needed a point to claim a 20th league title. It felt like they already had.

Those with a precious ticket for Liverpool v Spurs came to make Anfield vibrant. Those who didn't came for the party. And WHAT a party it was.

The queue for Taggy's Bar started at 9am. Next door on Anfield Road, Hotel TIA was chocca. By 2pm, the crowds lining the most famous road in football, excitedly waiting to greet the Liverpool FC team bus, were 20, 30, 40 deep. Any view was a good view. Scousers were back on their perches.

Scaffolding on a house next to Stanley Park became a giant climbing frame. Walls, signposts, lampposts, windowsills, roofs, the LFCTV Studio – if Kopites could clamber upon it to get a better view, they found a way.

Sir Kenny Dalglish's family stood on the Main Stand plaza, overseeing the spectacle like the LFC royalty they are. A drone beamed the pictures worldwide. Passengers on passing planes reached for smartphone cameras.

PRESS BOX:
BARNEY RONAY, THE GUARDIAN

"From the morning it felt like a flag day in the city, the streets dappled red, every corner thronged, like a street party for a republican coronation. You got to smell Anfield before you saw it, the tang of flares in the air as the crowd thickened into strolling families and tourists here just for the event glamour. At the Stanley Park end the pre-match smoke became a genuine peasouper, the Liverpool bus appearing like an icebreaker emerging out of the mist."

PUNDIT:
JAMIE REDKNAPP, SKY SPORTS

"When people say Liverpool made no major signings, the major signing was the manager. I spoke to Richard Hughes about this and I said 'why Arne Slot?' He said 'because everything pointed towards a man that could handle that big club mentality, you have to not just manage the team but you have to manage expectations. You have to be calm about managing this club.' I think the way that he has done that has been absolutely phenomenal."

HEAD COACH:
ARNE SLOT

"The only moment I was emotional today was when we arrived at the stadium – to see what it meant for the fans, what it meant for these people. I think everybody who was inside that bus felt that if the fans are with us, like they are, then it's impossible for us to lose this game of football. During the game, after the game, it's been incredible how the support of the fans were and how our players played. Special to be part of this day."

FOR THE RECORD:
Cody Gakpo became only the second Liverpool player to score in nine consecutive starts at Anfield after Mo Salah, who has achieved the feat twice.

ALSO THIS WEEKEND:
Chelsea 1-0 Everton
Bournemouth 1-1 Manchester United
Newcastle United 3-0 Ipswich Town

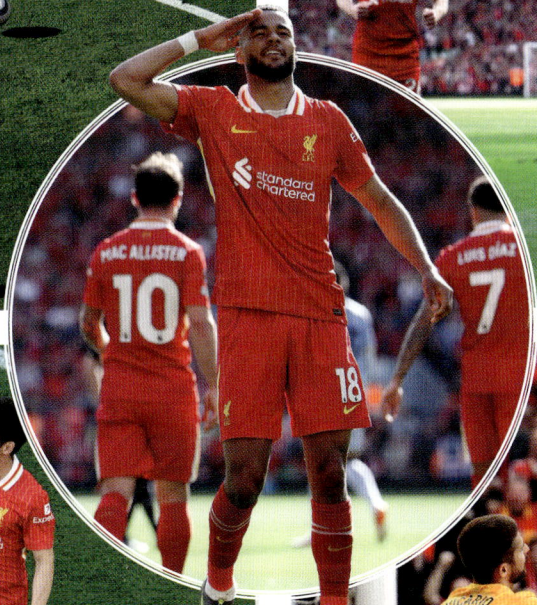

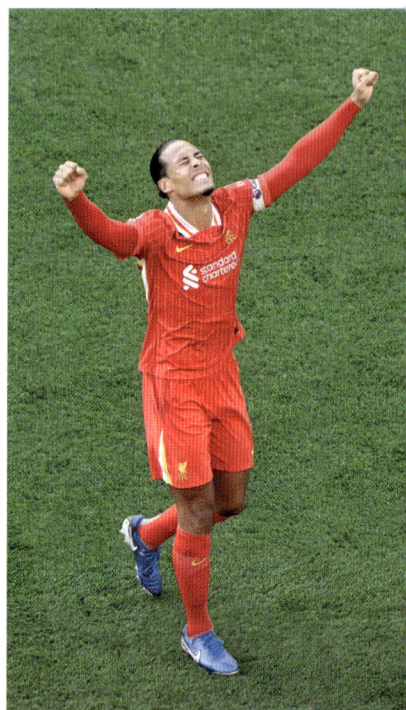

'Hand it over, hand it over, hand it over Manchester' rang out time and time again.

And the sunshine shone. It blazed down on the Red hordes. It was glorious. A perfect day to crown champions. And when the bus arrived the sky turned so red that, for a moment, as the sunlight peaked through the plumes of smoke, it was like an eerie red solar eclipse.

Normally, as Anfield fills up, the surrounding areas begin to empty. Not today. Those who couldn't find space inside the local hostelries peered through the windows or watched the match on their phones. The beer garden in The Sandon, a pub entwined in LFC history, resembled a pre-match fan park at a Champions League final.

The drinks flowed, anticipation built and inside Anfield, from an hour before kick-off, the noise grew, and grew and grew.

Kopites should have lived this day in 2020, when Jurgen Klopp's Reds ran away with the Premier League title, a first for 30 years. Coronavirus intervened, but even if it had happened fewer Reds would have seen it. The new Anfield Road Stand has since been

built and meant the crowd of 60,415 was a new Anfield record to witness a league title being won. And the Reds won in style.

'We're gonna win the league' rang around Anfield 15 minutes before kick-off. The pre-match communal signing of You'll Never Walk Alone was spine-tingling. Anfield was red. Anfield was loud. And amidst the countless scarves, some paying tribute to the 97, another Virgil quote, 'It Was Always Liverpool', was one of the many Kop banners.

Alisson had walked onto the pitch hand-in-hand with his children as mascots and the players did well to hear each other in the pre-match huddle. Over the course of the next two hours the Kop went through half of the Anfield Songbook. Fields of Anfield Road. Poor Scouser Tommy. Allez Allez Allez. Liverpool, Hallelujah! Hallelujah! The last line of A Liverbird Upon My Chest was adapted to 'and wins the championship today'.

Mo Salah curled the first shot on goal wide, Cody Gakpo's audacious overhead-kick went past the post. Then an old friend tried to play party pooper.

Dominic Solanke never scored at the Kop end during his 27-game

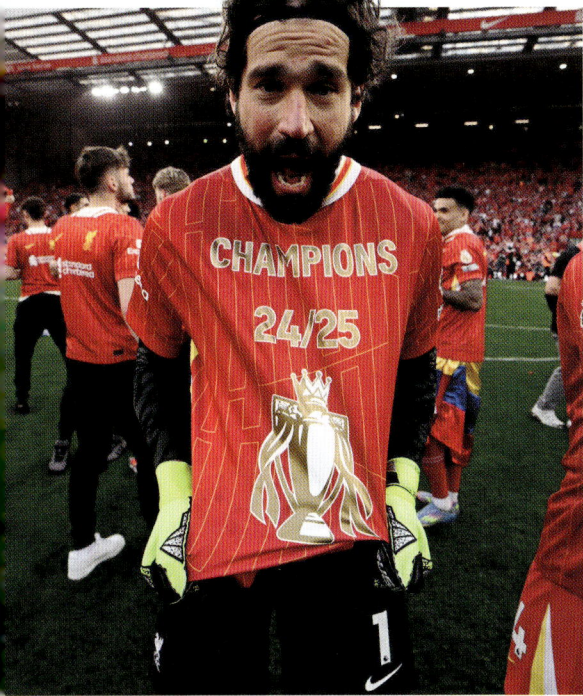

Liverpool career, but his 12th-minute header from a corner gave Spurs the lead and, briefly, pulled the plug on the surround sound.

Anfield responded with a wave of noise and Liverpool responded with a goal just four minutes later. Dominik Szoboszlai ran onto Salah's incisive pass and crossed for Luis Diaz to slide home. The assistant referee wanted to get in on the party-pooping act and raised his flag, but Diaz was owed a VAR decision against Spurs and Liverpool were level.

There was a tinge of relief in those celebrations, but not when Alexis Mac Allister fired the Reds ahead with a blistering left-footed strike from 22 yards out after Ryan Gravenberch tackled Archie Gray on the edge of the box.

A seismometer – an instrument that measures ground movement – had been installed under the Main Stand by liverpoolfc.com, with help from the University of Liverpool, and it recorded a peak magnitude 1.74 on the Richter scale after Mac Allister's goal. Anfield had created an actual seismic event, chants of 'And NOW Yer Gonna Believe Us' part of a tremendous tremor.

Maybe the ground was still moving when Mac Allister tried to take a 31st-minute corner. The ball wouldn't stay still, but when it was eventually delivered it was cleared to Gakpo, who side-stepped a couple of challenges before dispatching a low shot past Guglielmo Vicario to make it 3-1.

'We're Gonna Win The Football League Again' rang out and Spurs looked beaten. Spurs were beaten. "Once they got in front, with the atmosphere inside the stadium, it's fair to say it was going to be difficult for us," said Ange Postecoglou afterwards.

Ibrahima Konate prevented Mathys Tel from tapping home just before the interval and with the Reds having won 117 of their 119 Premier League matches when leading by two goals or more at half-time at Anfield, it was all about sealing title no.20 with style.

Liverpool had already had eight second-half shots before Salah made it 4-1 in the 63rd minute. Gravenberch won a tackle, Mac Allister and Szoboszlai drove forward, Salah cut inside onto his left foot and walloped a low shot past Vicario. He celebrated by running to the Kop, being handed a smartphone and taking a selfie.

Vicario prevented Szoboszlai from adding a fifth, but it soon came when Destiny Udogie tried to prevent Salah from converting

a Trent Alexander-Arnold cross, but turned the ball into his own net. It was Liverpool's first own goal of the season.

The final 20 minutes were simply a party. At one point referee Tom Bramall had to stop the game so a score of red balloons bobbling around on the pitch could be popped. Defiant chants of CHAMPIONS! CHAMPIONS! were bellowed for the first, but not last, time. Slot's name also rang out.

There was still time for Richarlison to get his customary Anfield booking after squabbling with Harvey Elliott, but with precisely 94 minutes and three seconds on the clock, and Slot already in a group hug with his staff, the referee blew the final whistle. Thus followed an explosion of noise, both inside and outside Anfield, that meant everything.

Joy. Relief. Exultation. Tears. Smiles. A whole gamut of emotions flowed through the bodies of every red. Finally, for the first time in front of the adoring Anfield support since 1990, Liverpool FC were champions. And it felt even better than you ever imagined it could.

'One Kiss' got the post-match celebrations going as the players embraced and group-hugged. A Kop banner simply said 'Gerrin There' while 'Back On Our Perch' was directed towards Manchester. A giant 'Champions' flag was unfurled above the Main Stand tunnel.

Slot's men ran to the Kop as a group more than once. Szoboszlai swung on the crossbar. Elliott waved a corner flag in the air and booted a ball into the Main Stand. Andy Robertson got the ball assistants, LFC Academy players, to join him and Virgil in a celebratory jig.

The Kop glowed red. Kids were hoisted onto shoulders. 'Freed

From Desire' got everyone bouncing. THIS is Anfield.

Kostas Tsimikas lifted a cardboard Premier League trophy cut-out aloft. Gravenberch took it for a dance. Konate was draped in a red 'Champions' flag. Mac Allister, the first to put on a 'Champions 24/25' shirt, waved to his wife to throw down his Argentina flag from the Sir Kenny Dalglish Stand. Alisson walked around shouting 'Champions!' before sitting on the pitch and sipping a Carlsberg. The Scousers in our team, Alexander-Arnold and Curtis Jones, shared a hug.

Virgil grabbed the match ball and, when YNWA was played, signalled for the entire squad and staff to line up in front of the Kop, arms around shoulders, for one of the most special, goosebump-inducing, emotional renditions Anfield has ever witnessed. Eyes misted over. Voices cracked. Imagine Being Us.

Outside the Paisley Gates, Walton Breck Road was a seething mass of red as a huge street party, that continued until the wee hours, gathered pace. The Twelfth Man, The Albert, The Park and Kop End Bar were rammed. You could smell the success.

Kopites called the players down to them, one-by-one, chanting their names before Slot addressed the crowd and paid tribute to his predecessor. 'Jurgen Klopp, na naa, na na na' he chanted as Robbo, Virgil, Harvey and Cody – wearing a scarf around his head like a school uniform tie on the last day of term – sprayed the boss with champagne. Slot even did Klopp-style fist-pumps for the Kop.

Three Little Birds sounded boss. So did Fields of Anfield Road. And as Not Nineteen Forever was aptly played, the Anfield scoreboards displayed those three little words.

Premier League Champions.

CHELSEA FC 3
LIVERPOOL FC 1

Goals: Fernandez (3), Quansah (56og), Van Dijk (85), Palmer (90+6pen)

04.05.25 · Stamford Bridge
Attendance: 39,829
Referee: Simon Hooper

CHELSEA (4-2-3-1): Sanchez, Caicedo, Chalobah, Colwill, Cucurella, Lavia (Gusto 78), Fernandez (C) (James 88), Neto, Palmer, Madueke, Jackson (Sancho 72). Subs not used: Jorgensen, Adarabioyo, Badiashile, Dewsbury-Hall, George, Acheampong. Booked: Chalobah.

LIVERPOOL (4-2-3-1): Alisson, Alexander-Arnold (Bradley 57), Quansah, Van Dijk (C), Tsimikas (Chiesa 82), Endo (Mac Allister 69), Jones, Salah, Elliott (Szoboszlai 69), Gakpo, Jota (Nunez 58). Subs not used: Kelleher, Konate, Diaz, Robertson. Booked: Van Dijk, Quansah.

PRESS BOX:
PHIL MCNULTY, BBC SPORT
"Liverpool were behind after three minutes, only really coming into their own after they fell two goals behind – substitute Nunez and Salah both missing big chances before Van Dijk briefly offered up the prospect of a late twist in the tale. None of this mattered to Liverpool's supporters, who celebrated their new status as Premier League champions throughout in their corner of Stamford Bridge, with an array of banners proudly marking their 20th title."

PUNDIT:
DAVID THOMPSON, LFCTV
"I thought Endo did alright today. He was one of the very few shining lights. He was passing the ball quickly. Other players were taking too many touches but he was on the one and two touch and whenever we did play the one and two touch we opened them up a bit. Taking too many touches and allowing them to get back

REPORT:
Forget the result, Liverpool supporters were made up in Chelsea as the Reds' title party continued in full swing at Stamford Bridge.

The game of football in front of them was a mere footnote for the 3,065 travelling Kopites in the Shed End. They danced in the concourse, they sang in the stands, they waved banners and balloons. Liverpool were champions and whatever happened on the pitch wasn't going to spoil the celebrations.

In the lower tier, a giant 'Champions Again' flag spanned almost the length of the entire section. Above it, red balloons spelt out the word Champions and the number 20. One banner featured the Premier League trophy, Champ20ns was above a retro club crest on another.

Draped from the top tier was a flag reading Slot's Appenin' Lad next to a Liver Bird. Imagine Being Us was also on display. Another simply

said 20, two giant silver balloons displayed the same magic numbers.

Song after song rang out – 'Campione, Campione, Campione Liverpool' must have got 20 airings – but it was a new tune celebrating the man who made it all possible that was on repeat.

"He brought us number 20 and his name is Arne Slot," they sang over and over again to Dutch party anthem 'Links Rechts', the tune that had Netherlands fans bouncing around the streets of Hamburg at UEFA Euro 2024.

It was a full-on title-winning party and in stark contrast to the welcome the players received from Chelsea's supporters, who booed the champions onto the pitch when their players sportingly gave Liverpool's starting XI a guard of honour.

Having won the league so early the Reds will have had more guards

into their shape was what was causing our own problems, but I thought Endo did well."

HEAD COACH: ARNE SLOT
"In general, a good performance, but the final percentages weren't there to win this game of football. In the lead-up to both goals a player of ours slipped. Would it have happened as well if the game was on the line? Yes or no, we will never know, but the margins are small in the Premier League, especially if you play a team like Chelsea with so many quality players, then you cannot afford these kinds of moments."

FOR THE RECORD:
Jarell Quansah's own goal was the first conceded by a Liverpool player at Stamford Bridge since Sander Westerveld in October 2000.

ALSO THIS WEEKEND:
Brentford 4-3 Manchester United
Arsenal 1-2 Bournemouth
Everton 2-2 Ipswich Town

of honour than Buckingham Palace by the end of the season, but on the evidence of this display they won't have many more points.

With the job done and the players having had a few days off to celebrate – and rightly so – there was a natural drop in intensity against Enzo Maresca's side, who needed to win to keep their hopes of Champions League qualification alive.

Liverpool's history is littered with a downturn in performances and results when a league has been won early – a reminder that coasting costs you at the top level, but also that it doesn't detract from winning a title. Unless anyone at Birmingham and Stoke in 1964, Bristol City in 1977 or Nottingham Forest and Watford in 1983 cares to disagree.

It took Chelsea just three minutes to score. Cole Palmer took advantage of a slip by Curtis Jones to burst through midfield and find Pedro Neto, who crossed for Enzo Fernandez to take a touch and slot the ball past Alisson.

Cody Gakpo had the Reds' only first-half shot on target, Robert Sanchez saving comfortably in the ninth minute, and although Diogo Jota and Trent Alexander-Arnold had efforts blocked it needed an offside flag against Nicolas Jackson to rule out a goal by Noni Madueke.

Liverpool presented the hosts with their second in the 56th minute. Palmer outfought Jones and beat Kostas Tsimikas to send in a low cross that Wataru Endo brilliantly prevented from being converted with a sliding challenge on Jackson, but when Virgil van Dijk tried to clear he smashed the ball into the net off Jarell Quansah.

Virgil headed a corner over, substitute Darwin Nunez completely misdirected a free header off target and Mo Salah also headed wide as the Reds finally found some zest, but Alisson also had to stop Jadon Sancho in a one-v-one before Palmer hit the inside of the post from a tight angle.

The Reds got a goal back when Van Dijk had another chance from an Alexis Mac Allister corner and this time headed home, but Liverpool's day was best summed up in stoppage time. Dominik Szoboszlai sloppily conceded possession, Quansah tripped Moises Caicedo in the box and as Palmer waited to take the penalty, all you could hear inside Stamford Bridge was a jubilant away end singing 'he brought us number 20 and his name is Arne Slot'.

"I always love seeing and hearing our away supporters, wherever we play, but the atmosphere and the noise you generated inside Stamford Bridge was really something," wrote Virgil in his Liverpool FC v Arsenal FC Official Matchday Programme notes a week later.

"It was spoken about in our dressing room after the game, that's for sure. We loved hearing our names sung, loved seeing how happy and joyful you all were."

Oh and by the way, Palmer scored and it finished 3-1.

LIVERPOOL FC v ARSENAL FC

REPORT:

"Bring on the champions," bellowed the Anfield crowd as Arsenal's players lined up in a guard of honour. It was first v second, but with the end-game already decided.

Back in the winter, it looked like this May meeting between the Reds and Gunners was potentially a title-decider, but when Arne Slot's team hit the accelerator Mikel Arteta's men tailed off.

They also arrived on Merseyside following a Champions League exit to PSG – an experience Liverpool had already lived – meaning a fifth consecutive season without silverware. So to walk into the next leg of Liverpool's Premier League title-winning party must have hurt and the Kop teased ex-Everton midfielder Arteta before kick-off with a banner depicting him as a bridesmaid.

Within four minutes his side, strangely wearing white shorts and socks with their black away shirts, should have led.

Conor Bradley conceded a free-kick and Liverpool tried to play the offside trap as Martin Odegaard took it, but Bukayo Saka ran from a deep position to bypass the Red line. He met the ball at the far post, but bobbled his shot across goal and wide.

Anfield was bathed in glorious sunshine and Liverpool looked in the mood to play football. A counter-attack in the eighth minute had such fluidity it was like lava was pouring forward. It didn't lead to a goal, David Raya getting down brilliantly to push Luis Diaz's shot away, but the Reds are hard to stop when they click and struck twice in quick succession.

Cody Gakpo raced onto Andy Robertson's pass but hesitated as he tried to find Mo Salah, allowing William Saliba to blast the ball over the touchline. Sharp as a tack, Curtis Jones took the throw-in quickly to the unmarked Robertson and with the Gunners having gone into standby mode he had time to pick out the unmarked Gakpo, who directed the ball past Raya with his head.

Anfield was still celebrating when Dominik

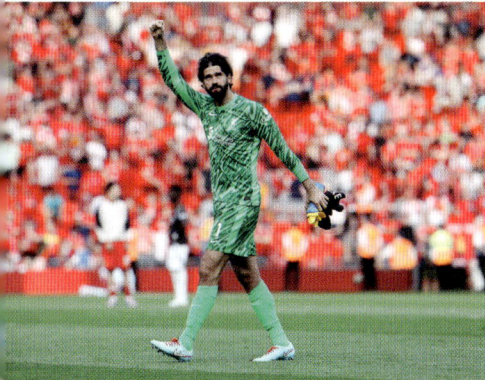

LIVERPOOL FC 2
ARSENAL FC 2

Goals: Gakpo (20), Diaz (21), Martinelli (47), Merino (70)

11.05.25 · Anfield · Attendance: 60,324

Referee: Anthony Taylor

LIVERPOOL (4-2-3-1): Alisson, Bradley (Alexander-Arnold 67), Konate, Van Dijk (C), Robertson, Gravenberch (Elliott 83), Jones (Nunez 67), Salah, Szoboszlai, Gakpo (Mac Allister 66), Diaz (Jota 79). Subs not used: Kelleher, Endo, Tsimikas, Quansah. Booked: Bradley.

ARSENAL (4-3-3): Raya, White (Calafiori 78), Saliba, Kiwior, Lewis-Skelly, Odegaard (C), Partey, Merino, Saka (Zinchenko 88), Trossard (Tierney 78), Martinelli. Subs not used: Neto, Timber, Sterling, Butler-Oyedeji, Henry-Francis, Nwaneri. Booked: Merino, Lewis-Skelly. Sent off: Merino (79).

PRESS BOX:
ANDY HUNTER, THE GUARDIAN
"Within seconds of the restart Liverpool regained possession and Salah swept a glorious pass between Kiwior and Myles Lewis-Skelly into the run of Szoboszlai. The midfielder squared beyond David Raya and Diaz slid in to apply the finishing touch. 'Best team in Europe? You're having a laugh,' sang the Kop, mocking Mikel Arteta's claims regarding his team's Champions League performance this season."

PUNDIT:
JAMIE CARRAGHER, SKY SPORTS
"Liverpool supporters think playing for Liverpool is the utmost and when you're a local player, like Trent is, like I was, you can't see yourself as bigger than the club. You've almost got to, not sacrifice yourself for the club, you're playing for Liverpool, it's a great honour, but you can never be seen to be almost bigger than the club, or better than the club. I always felt when I was playing, I wanted to be a one club man, I was determined to be that, but I always think, 'How do you leave Liverpool?' You can leave to join someone you think are better, but Liverpool supporters are not going to be happy with that."

HEAD COACH:
ARNE SLOT
"I think this is why people like the Premier League so much: two great teams that are competing with each other and a fantastic game of football. Both teams showing so much quality. Four goals, 2-2, both teams could have won it in the end. This is what makes the Premier League so special and this is also what we have to try as managers, not only to win games but also make sure the fans like what they see."

FOR THE RECORD:
Cody Gakpo scored in his 10th consecutive Anfield start, equalling Mo Salah's club record set in season 2017/18.

ALSO THIS WEEKEND:
Newcastle United 2-0 Chelsea
Manchester United 0-2 West Ham
Southampton 0-0 Manchester City

Szoboszlai ran onto Salah's defence-splitting pass and, with Raya tempted out of this goal into no-man's land, he squared for Diaz. Lucho could have tapped it in, but opted for his customary sliding finish so both he and the ball ended up in the back of the net.

The Colombian's goal came only a minute and 27 seconds after Gakpo's opener and prompted a bouquet of red balloons to float around Anfield. It was almost 3-0 two minutes later when another irresistible counter-attack ended with Jones curling a shot destined for the bottom corner until a full-stretch Raya fingertipped it past the post.

Between Mikel Merino getting cautioned for bringing down Bradley and Myles Lewis-Skelly following him into the book for about the umpteenth foul on Salah, Kopites questioned Arteta's midweek claim that there isn't a better team in Europe.

However, the Reds started the second half like the game had already finished and paid the price. Merino had a shot blocked by Gakpo seconds after the restart, but when Ryan Gravenberch gave the ball away, Leandro Trossard was invited to cross and Gabriel Martinelli, in so much space he must have had a VIP pass, glanced the ball in.

Alisson stopped Martinelli from doubling up when a free-kick was deflected into his path, but the Gunners were on top. Liverpool also looked a little rattled when Trent Alexander-Arnold, who'd announced he'd be leaving LFC when his contract expires in June, was given a mixed reaction when brought on for Bradley.

Arsenal equalised in the 70th minute. Odegaard's venomous 25-yard strike was magnificently tipped onto the post by Alisson, but Merino reacted the quickest to convert the rebound with a diving header.

Gravenberch fired a shot wide before the game swung back in Liverpool's favour when the already-booked Merino lost possession on the edge of his box, tripped Diaz and followed it up by scything down Szoboszlai. It was adios to Merino and Alexander-Arnold curled the free-kick narrowly wide.

Liverpool flowed forward again like in the opening half-hour. Jota sliced a shot across goal and Robertson volleyed a Darwin Nunez flick-on wide with the net begging to be hit.

A stray Harvey Elliott pass gave Odegaard a chance to win it, but he was also off target, and in stoppage time Robertson thought he'd bagged a dramatic winner from close range after Raya somehow kept out Van Dijk's header from a corner, but Konate had fouled Lewis-Skelly.

So the champions had to settle for a point, but having made this match meaningless in the title race they'd already won.

BRIGHTON & HOVE ALBION FC 3
LIVERPOOL FC 2

Goals: Elliott (9), Ayari (32), Szoboszlai (45+1), Mitoma (69), Hinshelwood (85)

19.05.25 · AMEX Stadium
Attendance: 31,611
Referee: Andy Madley

BRIGHTON (4-2-3-1): Verbruggen, Wieffer, Van Hecke, Webster, Estupinan, Baleba, Ayari (D Gomez 74), Minteh (Hinshelwood 84), Gruda (O'Riley 73), Adingra (Mitoma 65), Welbeck (C) (Howell 84). Subs not used: Rushworth, Igor Julio, Dunk, Veltman. Booked: Webster.

LIVERPOOL (4-2-3-1): Alisson, Bradley (Endo 77), Konate, Quansah, Tsimikas, Gravenberch, Szoboszlai (Jones 63), Salah (C), Elliott, Gakpo (Diaz 63), Chiesa (Nunez 63). Subs not used: Kelleher, J Gomez, Van Dijk, Robertson, Alexander-Arnold.

PRESS BOX:
PAUL GORST, LIVERPOOL ECHO
"You can file this 3-2 loss at Brighton alongside Chelsea, the Champions League dead rubber at PSV and the first-leg semi-final hiccup at Tottenham as results that haven't really carried much weight in the grander scheme of things. This latest setback certainly meant little to those in the away end here at the AMEX who, by the end of the game, had given up the pretence of being concerned about the outcome, declaring instead that this week is really about what is to come on Sunday."

PUNDIT:
DIDI HAMANN, NOW SPORTS TV
"Details and little margins decide games and if you haven't got the last two or three percent of urgency, which they haven't had for the last two or three games because they're champions, then you lose these games. If Liverpool needed to win this game maybe we would have seen a different outcome. Credit to Brighton, they had to win and turned the game around, but it was probably a good time to play Liverpool."

REPORT:
After seeing social media footage of Arne Slot celebrating in Ibiza and much of his squad enjoying themselves in Dubai having been given some time off before this Monday night fixture, Liverpool supporters wondered if the Redmen would turn up at Brighton wearing Hawaiian shorts and bucket hats.

When Mo Salah – captaining the Reds for the first time in a Premier League fixture – led his team out through the Seagulls' guard of honour he wasn't clutching glow-sticks, but with Slot admitting in his pre-match press conference that it is hard to motivate a team that are already champions it was an opportunity for Fabian Hurzeler's men.

Brighton needed to win to maintain hopes of European qualification and with some travelling Kopites wearing party hats and blowing up balloons as they got the new Federico Chiesa song ringing around the concourse before kick-off, all that was missing was a buffet on the touchline and a pinata hanging from the crossbar.

Chiesa was handed his first league start of the season in a central forward role with Virgil van Dijk and Luis Diaz rested, while Alexis Mac Allister and Diogo Jota got the night off. Joe Gomez was back on the bench after three months out injured.

What followed was a fantastic game of flowing football with 43 shots on goal – 17 of them on target – and five goals. There could easily have been more.

HEAD COACH:
ARNE SLOT

"A great game of football. Two teams that wanted to play, two teams that wanted to win, had no intentions to do things that people normally don't like to see, no time-wasting, no tumbling. Two teams that were just for almost 100 minutes trying to win a game of football and with some brilliant individual moments. I saw many things that I already knew and one of them is how close the margins have been throughout our whole season. And now with us failing to score the third, with us just missing maybe this two or three per cent sometimes in our defensive work, immediately it leads to us losing games of football."

FOR THE RECORD:
Liverpool became the first team in Premier League history to score two or more goals in 31 games of a season.

ALSO THIS WEEKEND:
Everton 2-0 Southampton
Arsenal 1-0 Newcastle United
Chelsea 1-0 Manchester United

Liverpool started well with Cody Gakpo bending a shot past the upright after Dominik Szoboszlai drove forward. Conor Bradley, who had signed a new contract two days prior, was a constant threat down the right and in the ninth minute he created the opening goal.

Salah, making his 400th LFC appearance, guided Szoboszlai's pass into his path and Bradley nutmegged Simon Adringa to get into the box, dropped his shoulder to wrongfoot Adam Webster and pulled the ball back for Harvey Elliott to score from five yards. For the first time, the Reds had scored in every away league match in a single season.

Bradley was starting a Premier League game for just the 16th time of his Liverpool career and should have netted his first goal away from Anfield when he side-footed Chiesa's pass beyond the far post with only Bart Verbruggen to beat.

Brighton had more possession and after Danny Welbeck headed wide from six yards out they drew level. Brajan Gruda clipped a pass over a static Reds defence and Yasin Ayari beat Alisson from the edge of the box. 1-1.

Pervis Estupinan obstructed another Bradley run down the right in first-half stoppage time and with Brighton detailing nine players to mark six Reds in the box, and only Yankuba Minteh in front of them, Szoboszlai and Elliott played it short.

Szoboszlai found himself in enough space on the right to graze sheep, and he was looking sheepish seconds later when he pinged an attempted cross over Verbruggen. It was a stunning goal, even if he didn't mean it, and Szoboszlai celebrated by shoving the ball up his shirt and sucking his thumb to signal a new arrival is on the way.

Welbeck forced Alisson into a sprawling save from a free-kick after the break before Chiesa had a shot blocked. When Jarell Quansah ended a Brighton counter-attack with a fine challenge it allowed the Reds to counter their counter.

Kostas Tsimikas released Gakpo, who burst past Mats Wieffer despite having his shirt pulled, before delivering a cross for Salah. Six yards out, in front of a near open goal, Salah scores 99 times out of 100, but this was the one he missed, angling his shot wide.

At the other end, Alisson made a top-class save by flying off his line to deny Welbeck with an imposing block while Salah's next effort was brilliantly clawed out by Verbruggen after more good work by Bradley.

A goal was coming, but it was Brighton who got it. Alisson beat away another Welbeck strike, but the ball looped up for substitute Kaoru Mitoma and he scored with a bouncing shot.

Both sides traded attacks, but it was Jack Hinshelwood who struck the decisive blow when he converted Matt O'Riley's cross at the back stick, the goal given after VAR overruled an initial offside call.

You'd have thought Liverpool had won judging by the away end, the travelling Kop bouncing around to Freed From Desire at full-time, but then defeats are easier to accept when you're being presented with the Premier League trophy six days later. Bring on the champions...

CHAMPIONS 2024/25

LIVERPOOL FC 1
CRYSTAL PALACE FC 1

Goals: Sarr (9), Salah (84)
25.05.25 · Anfield · Attendance: 60,382
Referee: Darren England

LIVERPOOL (4-2-3-1): Alisson, Bradley (Alexander-Arnold 46), Konate (Jota 62), Van Dijk (C), Robertson (Elliott 85), Gravenberch, Jones, Salah, Szoboszlai (Nunez 61), Diaz (Endo 69), Gakpo. Subs not used: Kelleher, Gomez, Tsimikas, Quansah. Booked: Gravenberch, Van Dijk. Sent-off: Gravenberch (69).

CRYSTAL PALACE (3-4-2-1): Henderson (C), Richards, Lacroix, Lerma, Munoz, Hughes (Esse 79 (Franca 90+3)), Kamada, Mitchell, Sarr, Eze (Devenny 62), Mateta (Nketiah 62). Subs not used: Turner, Ward, Kporha.

REPORT:

Today was the day. Thirty-five years on since Alan Hansen lifted the Football League trophy aloft at Anfield came the moment every Kopite, young and old, had waited for.

Liverpool FC were being crowned as Premier League champions and over 60,000 were at Anfield to see it.

Jordan Henderson received the glittering Premier League trophy from Sir Kenny Dalglish on an empty Kop in 2020 when the pandemic stopped the turnstiles from clicking, while the only captain to previously lift it in front of a full house at Anfield was Blackburn's Tim Sherwood back in 1995 when King Kenny was Rovers manager, but now it was time for a proper coronation.

Virgil van Dijk, the cornerstone of Jürgen Klopp's revolution and Arne Slot's evolution, had the responsibility – the privilege – of being the man who would receive Liverpool FC's 20th league title. And while Liverpudlians had spent the season singing 'hand it over, Manchester', the skipper had someone else in mind.

"I was determined to make sure that Alan Hansen was going to be the one who handed it to me. I suggested it and I'm glad it worked out. I was really happy for him that he also got his moment with the cup because he's one of the greatest centre-backs this club has seen and totally deserved his moment in front of the Kop."

PRESS BOX:
CHRIS BASCOMBE, DAILY TELEGRAPH
"Liverpool could finally stop chasing the Premier League trophy and start dancing with it. After three decades of dreaming, and four weeks of rehearsals in the gratifying knowledge a date was circled in the diary, Anfield's red letter day arrived. Once the prize was unveiled it shimmered like a mirrorball, enabling skipper Virgil van Dijk to see the reflections of the Kop gods who have reserved him a seat in their VIP lounge. Most prominent, of course, was former captain Alan Hansen, who led the presentation committee, serenaded by the Kop as if he was in his prime."

PUNDIT:
ALAN SHEARER, BBC MATCH OF THE DAY
"Mo Salah - what a season, what a player. Twenty-nine goals in the league and 18 assists, it's just ridiculous consistency from this guy. He very rarely misses any games and he brings brilliance to Liverpool. Once he gets onto his left foot he's deadly. He's an incredible player who obviously plays in a very good team, but good teams need great players. There's no doubt that he is that, he's been sensational."

HEAD COACH: ARNE SLOT
"I think I could feel today that it was 35 years ago that the fans were part of a day like today. It's only been five years ago that we won the league, but unfortunately the fans couldn't be there. Now they were and I think everybody could see what it means for the fans to win it, and that is what makes it special and, in the end, for us as well. Because you play football for yourself, for your family, but definitely also for the fans, and we are privileged that we can play it in front of them because these ones are special."

FOR THE RECORD:
Mo Salah became only the second Liverpool player to finish as leading scorer in eight consecutive seasons after club record-holder Roger Hunt (1961/62 - 1968/69).

ALSO THIS WEEKEND:
Nottingham Forest 0-1 Chelsea
Newcastle United 0-1 Everton
Southampton 1-2 Arsenal

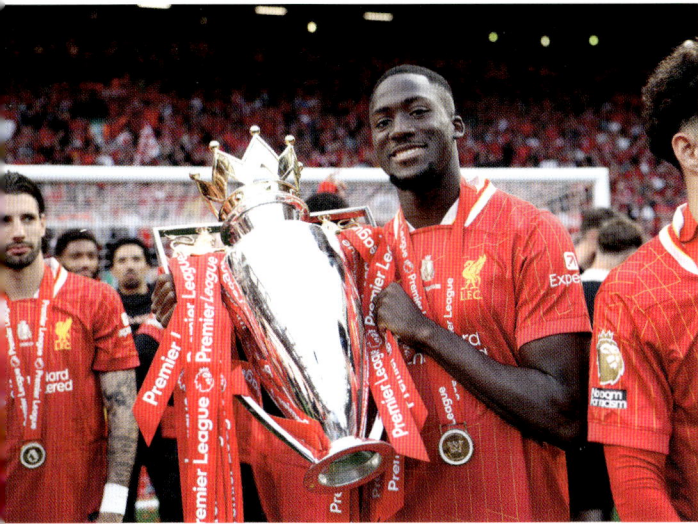

The pair later posed for an iconic photo, supporters chanting Hansen's name like he was a current player. It was far from the only moment of respect at a stadium bubbling with anticipation and excitement hours before kick-off.

Outside the Shankly Gates, the Liverpool team bus arrived via Arkles Lane and received an incredible reception as thousands lined the streets. And when the Reds emerged onto the Anfield pitch through Crystal Palace's guard of honour the noise that greeted the champions was phenomenal.

A mosaic, that began in the Lower Anfield Road Stand and ended in the Kop, read LFC CAMPIONE 20, and among the flags being waved between the red and white cards upon football's most famous stand was a striking red and white banner, split into two sections and quoting a Kop anthem: A Team That Plays The Liverpool Way And Wins The Championship In May.

Another banner on the Kop quoted Bill Shankly – Liverpool FC Exists To Win Trophies – as did one in the Lower Sir Kenny Dalglish Stand: This Is Our Bread And Butter.

Yet Liverpool weren't the only trophy-winning team at Anfield and to congratulate the Eagles on their maiden FA Cup final victory against Manchester City – the first major trophy win in Crystal Palace's history – the Redmen lined up in their own guard of honour.

It was a moment of pure, authentic sportsmanship and the applause and cheers of both sets of supporters, who will meet again for the first game of next season in the FA Community Shield at Wembley, was heartfelt.

Jürgen Klopp, dressed in a smart suit and back at Anfield for his first Premier League game since stepping down, was captured on camera in the Main Stand saying 'wow' as he clapped along. Later on he was singing along to the Mo Salah song, like any other Kloppite, but before a ball was kicked came another spine-tingling pre-match singing of You'll Never Walk Alone after the man who plays it, George Sephton, received a shirt from Sir Kenny on the pitch to mark his retirement after 54 years as LFC stadium announcer. Anfield matchdays will never sound the same again.

With Rafa Benitez and Roy Evans, plus Phil Thompson, Ian Rush, ➡

Steven Gerrard – on the 20th anniversary of Istanbul – and Jordan Henderson among those in attendance, Liverpool could've filled a row with ex-managers and captains, but after an opening eight minutes in which the match felt like a case of 'before the Lord Mayor's Show', Palace took the lead.

Conor Bradley's pass was intercepted by Tyrick Mitchell and with the gap between Virgil and Ibrahima Konate almost as big as the gap between Liverpool and Manchester United – a top-flight record 42 points by the end of the day – he played Ismaila Sarr in to stroke the ball past Alisson.

It didn't stop Liverpool supporters from singing, and the referee stopped play briefly to allow a bouquet of red balloons that had invaded the pitch to be popped with Cody Gakpo showing great technique, but it was the 26th minute before the Reds threatened Dean Henderson's goal, Luis Diaz cutting inside and bending a shot past the far post.

Lucho also headed a Ryan Gravenberch cross over before Jean-Philippe Mateta had a goal disallowed for a clear offside. The Frenchman also hit the crossbar, but again the assistant's flag was waving.

Diaz came even closer three minutes later when he spun to let Salah's chipped pass drop over his shoulder before striking a first-time half-volley with his left foot, but Eagles goalie Henderson deflected the ball through his own legs with his right boot and wide of the post, much to the frustration of the Colombian, who kicked the post.

Arne Slot acted decisively at half-time and brought on Trent

Alexander-Arnold for Bradley, the mixed reaction he received at the Arsenal game replaced with cheers. It ensured Alexander-Arnold got the send-off his trophy-laden 354-game LFC career merits and was good to see.

Trent was Liverpool's best player in the second period, whipping in a couple of delicious crosses in the opening 10 minutes that nobody got on the end of, prompting Slot to withdraw Konate and Dominik Szoboszlai for Diogo Jota and Darwin Nunez.

Gravenberch, Premier League Young Player of the Year, dropped back to play as a right-sided centre-half as part of the tactical tweak, but moments after Alexander-Arnold played Nunez in, only for Henderson to spread himself like a starfish to save, came a setback.

A Liverpool cross was cleared and as Gravenberch, still the last man back for a corner taken seconds earlier, tried to control the ball he slipped and took out Daichi Kamada. It was close to the halfway line, but with only Alisson behind him it was a clear goalscoring opportunity and the Dutch international, who had already been booked, was shown a straight red card.

Wataru Endo was brought on for Diaz but despite going down to 10 men the Reds continued to enjoy more possession and when Andy Robertson picked out Gakpo with a lovely pass he pulled the ball back to Jota, who scuffed a shot past Henderson but stuck the post.

Oliver Glasner's men looked on course to make it consecutive 1-0 Anfield wins, but Salah still needed a goal or an assist to equal the Premier League record of 47 goal involvements – set by Andrew Cole (1994) and Alan Shearer (1995) – and in the 84th minute Palace became the 20th different team he has scored against this season.

Jota won a tackle in the right-back position and launched a ball forward that Mitchell could only head to Salah. It went back to Jota, who had sprinted forward, and he found Nunez on the right.

Nunez crossed to the far post, Gakpo headed back across goal and Salah arrived to strike a karate-kick half-volley that flew into the net via the arm of Maxence Lacroix.

A goal from the FWA Footballer of the Year and Premier League Player of the Year was a fitting way for Liverpool's title-winning campaign to end – 'ee-aye-addio, we've won the league' echoing out at full-time – and it was Salah who got his hands on a couple of trophies first.

Ian Rush presented the Egyptian King with the Premier League Golden Boot and Premier League Playmaker of the Season awards for the most goals and assists. It was further due recognition for another stellar Salah season, but the moment every Red had waited so long for was still to come.

A podium as purple as a Scouse wheelie bin was constructed in the centre circle and a huge Champions banner laid out behind it. Photographers congregated on a ramp and, again at the request of the captain, Mark and Joanne McVeigh of the Owen McVeigh Foundation brought the trophy out.

Weighing 25.4kg – four stone – the Premier League trophy is more than three times heavier than the European Cup, but 15.9kg of that weight is contained in the green and silver removable base. Made from malachite, a precious stone largely found in Africa, it was freshly engraved with '2024-25 LIVERPOOL FC' upon it.

Standing at 3ft 5ins tall, the trophy itself is made of sterling silver and was cast by Asprey London – the Crown Jewellers – with the design based on the Three Lions that represent English football. Two of the golden lions can be found above the handles on either side of the trophy and, according to the Premier League: "when the captain of the title-winning team raises the trophy, and its gold crown, above his head he becomes the third lion."

Before Virgil became the mane man, Slot and his players emerged back onto the pitch through a champions arch. The Liverpool FC head coach stepped onto the podium first, applauding supporters and punching the air before getting his winner's medal and a hug from Hansen.

Each of his players, wearing their special Champions 24/25 shirts, followed to get their medals and had their names cheered one by one as announcer Peter McDowall read them out.

"Harvey Davies. Tyler Morton. Alisson Becker. Cody Gakpo. Ibrahima Konate. Dominik Szoboszlai. Curtis Jones. Wataru Endo. Vitezslav Jaros. Harvey Elliott. Federico Chiesa. Joe Gomez. Andrew Robertson. Conor Bradley. Jarell Quansah. Ryan Gravenberch. Caoimhin Kelleher. Diogo Jota. Luis Diaz. Alexis Mac Allister. Darwin Nunez. Kostas Tsimikas. Trent Alexander-Arnold. Mo Salah. And your captain, Virgil van Dijk."

You could hear the anticipation building as Hansen slipped a medal around Virgil's neck before Liverpool's 1990 title-winning captain handed the Premier League trophy to Liverpool's 2025 title-winning captain. Hello, hello, here we go.

The Dutch colossus walked towards his team-mates, some of them crouching and shaking their arms, others bouncing at the back, and with a bend of his knees, while facing the Main Stand, Virgil lifted that beautiful piece of shimmering silverware above his head to make the dreams of all those Reds inside Anfield, and all those watching around the world, come true. CHAMPIONS!

D

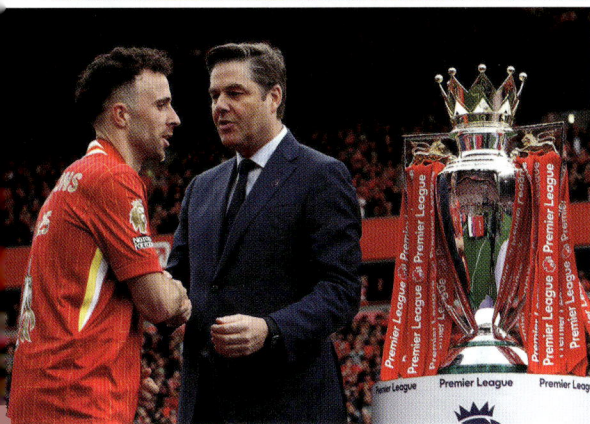

Ticker-tape cannons blasted out red confetti, jets of flames burned brightly upwards and fireworks made the sky glow rouge as 'Campione, Campione' rang out. In the stands, those chants, cheers and hugs were mixed with tears trickling down cheeks. The wait was over. Liverpool were FC Twenty. And Anfield was brimming with emotion.

Slot, ever the modest man, stood aside as his players celebrated in front of the cameras. Each player took it in turns to lift the trophy as the red ribbons fluttered in the breeze and fireworks crackled among the clouds. You could barely see Anfield from above through the smoke.

Liverpool's trophy anthem, One Kiss, was first to be played over the PA system as Slot's backroom staff and younger squad players, including James McConnell with his foot in a protective boot, arrived on the podium to join the first-teamers.

Alisson whipped off his top to reveal a black t-shirt celebrating his faith. Alexander-Arnold placed the trophy's crown upon Salah's head before it was fixed back on to the trophy by the Liverpool 'keeper so Gakpo could have his turn. Thanks, Dad.

It was Alisson who set off on a mazy run down towards the Kop, clutching the trophy before leaping into the air in front of his goal as supporters hollered in delight. Gakpo swung from the crossbar and before long Alisson was sitting on it, continuing to lead the celebrations. Champions! Champions! Champions!

Various players had their names sung, but when cult-hero Chiesa's chant went up the place was rocking. His team-mates surrounded the Italian and bounced around before clearing a space for Slot to pick up the trophy and, on the edge of the six yard box, he hoisted it towards the Kop to huge cheers.

Just like after the Spurs game, Freed From Desire provided the backing for some of the wildest celebrations with the trophy raised by the skipper in the midst of a massive bouncing huddle of joy.

The Liverpool squad lined up, arm-in-arm, in front of the Kop for another special rendition of You'll Never Walk Alone and Slot took the trophy over to principal owner John W Henry, chairman Tom Werner, FSG president Mike Gordon and their families for photos as Not Nineteen Forever reminded everyone of how things can change.

With the players' families joining the celebrations, a lap of honour followed before Virgil instructed the entire squad – some of them abandoning media interviews mid-chat – to congregate again in front of the Kop for a group photo.

Prior to the game, Van Dijk had also arranged for a photo of everyone who works at the AXA Training Centre, from coaching staff and players to chefs and receptionists, to be taken for publication in the Matchday Programme. That, in a nutshell, has always been the secret of Liverpool's success over the years. It's collective.

Owners, coaches, players, staff, supporters – each plays an integral part and the result of all their efforts in 2024/25 is now displayed on the Champions Wall: 20.

But we are Liverpool and we're never gonna stop.

Yes, twenty is plenty, but if Arne Slot and his champions come back next season even stronger then twenty-one is on.

D

VIRGIL VAN DIJK

"It was very emotional. A special day. A special day for my mum, my wife, my kids. It's incredible to be champions and no-one can take this one away from us. Obviously I chose this club because I felt like it could happen, I felt this connection. I love this club, I love the fans, I love what Liverpool stands for. I'm really happy that I've extended [my contract] for two years. The love doesn't go unnoticed, so keep going.

"Having been denied this in 2020, we all had a duty today to make the most of this opportunity, and to make it the most happy and joyful experience possible. We have to enjoy these moments, because these are the things we work for, every single day. We sacrifice a lot as players, believe me, but all those long days and cold nights, those near misses and disappointments, those brilliant performances and last-minute winners, it's all worth it when you get a day like today."

MOHAMED SALAH

"It's incredible, incredible. Last time we didn't have a chance to do it in front of the Kop. Today we had a chance. It's an incredible feeling to win the Premier League for this club. I don't think I've ever heard the fans so loud. Last time, we won it in the pandemic so it wasn't really a great feeling. But still the Premier League. Winning the second one with the fans in Anfield, especially the Spurs game and now... you can see what it means."

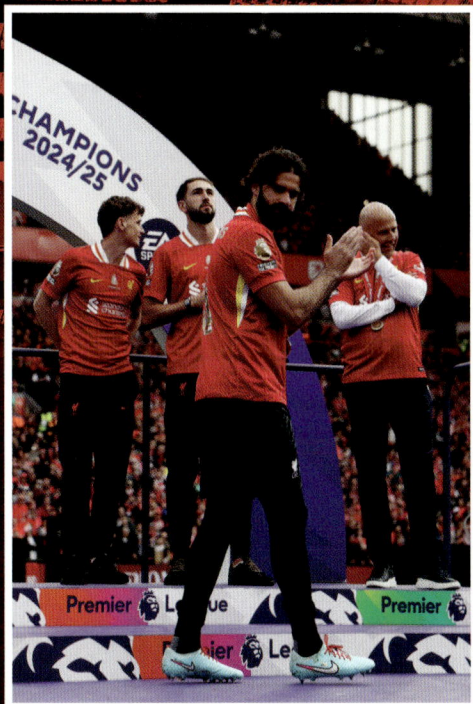

ALISSON

"We had a full house today to celebrate in front of our fans. They are a massive part of this club, I think the main part of this club. Everything we do, we don't do it not for ourselves or for our families - of course we have individual ambitions and ambitions as a team - but every time we go onto the pitch and we work so hard, we do that for them as well. So, nothing is more fair that we could enjoy and celebrate in front of them. It makes everything more special."

ANDY ROBERTSON

"It feels like a long wait to finally get your hands on it. Getting the trophy is always so special. We've obviously won it early so it has felt like an age still for it to come around. But seeing Virg lift it and just being able to lift it in front of the fans finally for a long wait, it's a special day."

RYAN GRAVENBERCH

"It's really amazing. If you saw the fans… it's really nice to have this moment. I'm proud I'm here and can be in this moment. To be honest, I'm really happy with my season. I think nobody talked before the season that I was capable of doing this, and I'm happy that I could show myself again."

CURTIS JONES

"It doesn't get much better. I've worked all year for this, the whole of my life for it. And just to be a part of this team and a part of this club, I'm just grateful – so grateful. It's better [than in 2020] because I've played even more games so now it feels like I've been a big part of the team and a part of the squad. That's what it's all about, the team. At the end of the year, if we come away with cups and trophies, that's what it's all about. There's been times when I could have moaned or could have sulked when I thought I should have played more games – but I don't care. It's just all about the team. I'm a Scouser, I've come all the way through and I'm here. I'm just taking it all in."

ALEXIS MAC ALLISTER

"It's so, so special. This club deserves it. When I arrived at this club, I said I was here to win trophies and this is maybe the biggest one you can get here. I'm really, really happy but I'm pretty sure that this is just the beginning."

CODY GAKPO

"Amazing feeling, amazing experience with the fans. Difficult to describe. It's more special because everybody is here, you can feel the atmosphere - it's amazing and we are going to enjoy it."

CAOIMHIN KELLEHER

"It's obviously really special, a nice atmosphere in the whole crowd. I've made a few appearances this season as well, so it's nice to win something at the end of the season. It's special memories for us all, we just soak up the atmosphere."

CONOR BRADLEY

"It's hard to put into words, the scenes that have just happened, it's just so special. To do it with the club I've supported all my life makes it even more special. I'm just on top of the world. When I moved over at 16, I didn't imagine any of this was possible. To even just be here, I'm so proud."

HARVEY ELLIOTT

"I can't really put it into words, to be honest. It's just an unbelievable experience, looking around the whole stadium, the celebrations, the enjoyment. Even outside the stadium, I'm looking forward to seeing all the scenes out there. The first time, it was COVID so we couldn't really celebrate properly but now we are able to celebrate with the fans and we're able to experience all of this. It's going to be a long night but it's just incredible, it's unbelievable."

TRENT ALEXANDER-ARNOLD

"I'll remember these moments for the rest of my life, especially a day like today. It goes down as the best day for me in my life. A very, very special day and a very special achievement for the team and for the club."

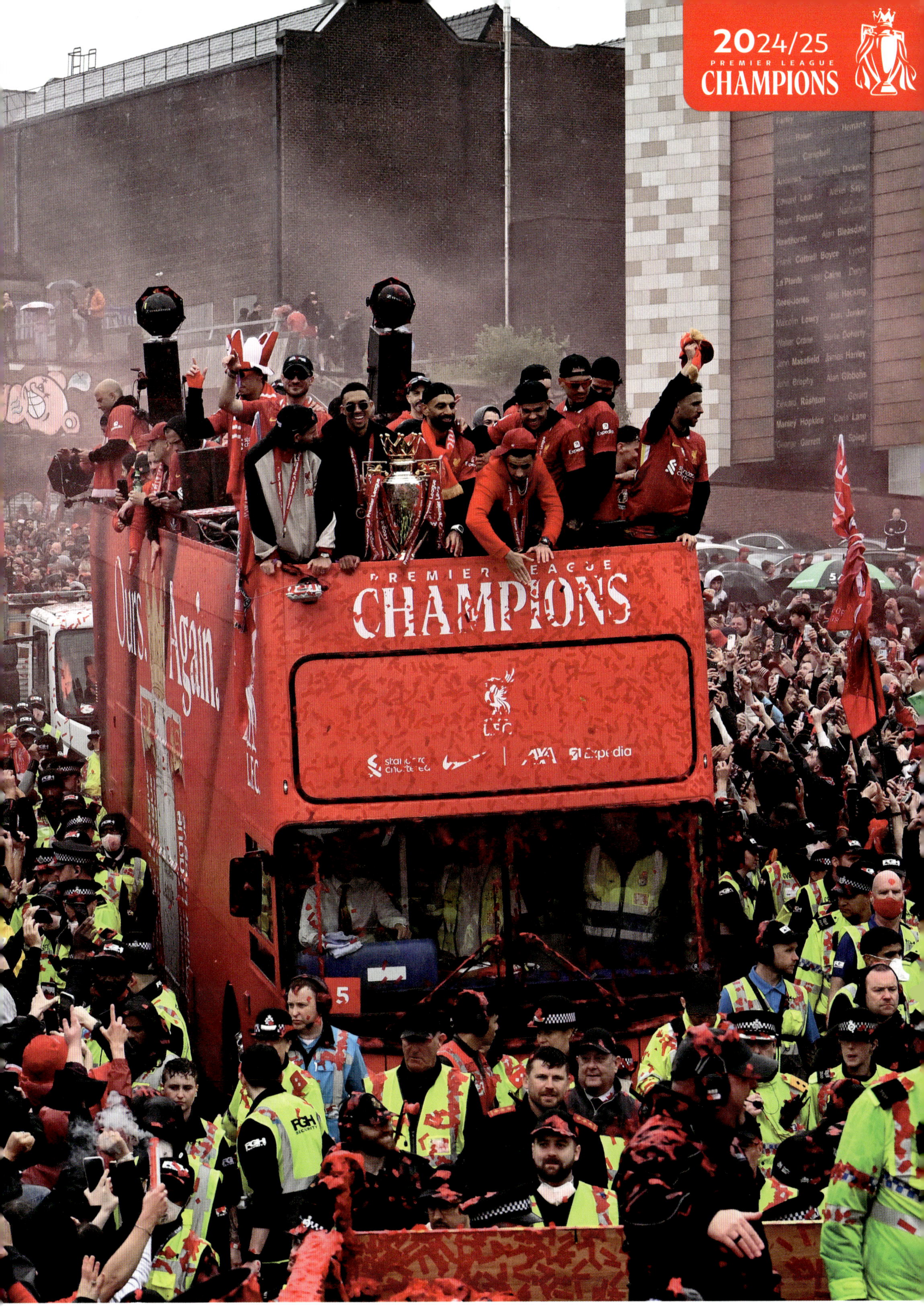
PREMIER LEAGUE
CHAMPIONS
Ours. Again.
LFC
Expedia

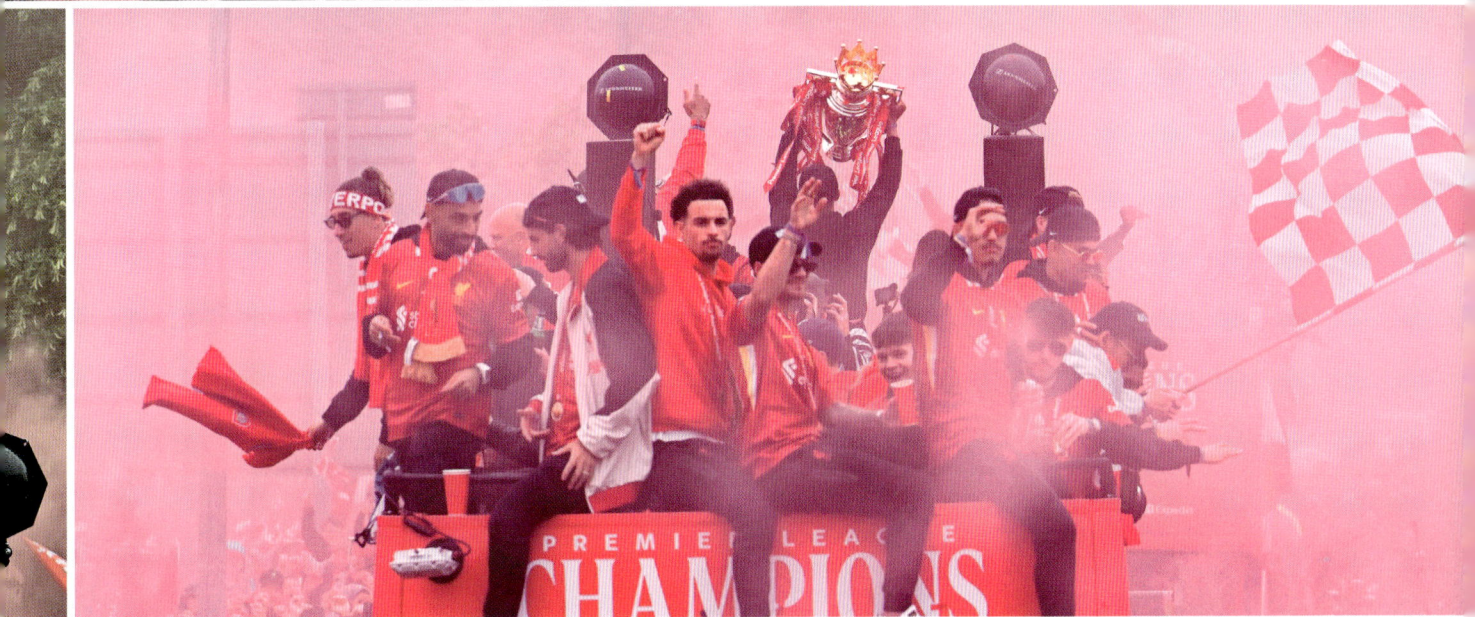

Main image: Cunard

LIVERPOOL FC 2024/25 PREMIER LEAGUE STATISTICS

PLAYER STATS

NAME	APP	G	A	CS*	Y/R
Mo Salah	38	29	18	8	1/0
Virgil van Dijk	37	3	1	14	5/0
Ryan Gravenberch	37	0	4	11	6/1
Luis Diaz	36	13	5	4	2/0
Dominik Szoboszlai	36	6	6	8	6/0
Alexis Mac Allister	35	5	5	9	6/0
Cody Gakpo	35	10	4	1	5/0
Trent Alexander-Arnold	33	3	6	4	5/0
Andy Robertson	33	0	1	6	3/1
Curtis Jones	33	3	3	1	1/1
Ibrahima Konate	31	1	2	11	5/0
Darwin Nunez	30	5	2	0	8/0
Alisson	28	0	0	10	0/0
Diogo Jota	26	6	3	1	2/0
Wataru Endo	20	0	0	0	0/0
Conor Bradley	19	0	2	0	4/0
Kostas Tsimikas	18	0	1	2	2/0
Harvey Elliott	18	1	2	0	1/0
Jarell Quansah	13	0	0	0	2/0
Caoimhin Kelleher	10	0	0	4	0/0
Joe Gomez	9	0	0	1	1/0
Federico Chiesa	6	0	0	0	0/0
Vitezslav Jaros	1	0	0	1	0/0
Jayden Danns	1	0	0	0	0/0
Own Goals	-	1	-	-	-

APP - GAMES, G - GOALS, A - ASSISTS
CS - CLEAN SHEETS
Y/R - YELLOW / RED CARDS

*outfield players must have been on for at least 60 minutes to be awarded a clean sheet

ANFIELD PREMIER LEAGUE ATTENDANCES 2024/25

OPPONENT	ATT
Ipswich Town	60,420
Tottenham Hotspur	60,415
Wolverhampton Wanderers	60,401
Southampton	60,399
Crystal Palace	60,382
West Ham United	60,376
Newcastle United	60,374
AFC Bournemouth	60,347
Nottingham Forest	60,344
Fulham	60,333
Brighton & Hove Albion	60,331
Everton	60,331
Arsenal	60,324
Leicester City	60,300
Aston Villa	60,292
Chelsea	60,277
Manchester United	60,275
Manchester City	60,248
Brentford	60,107
Average	**60,330**

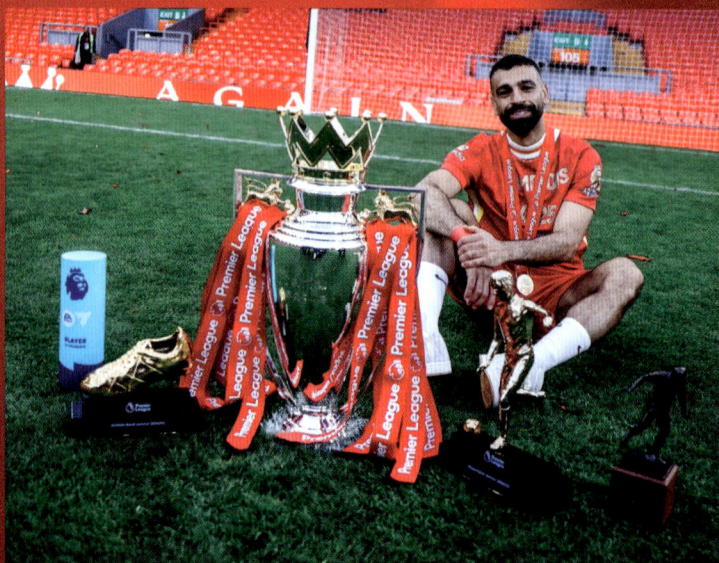

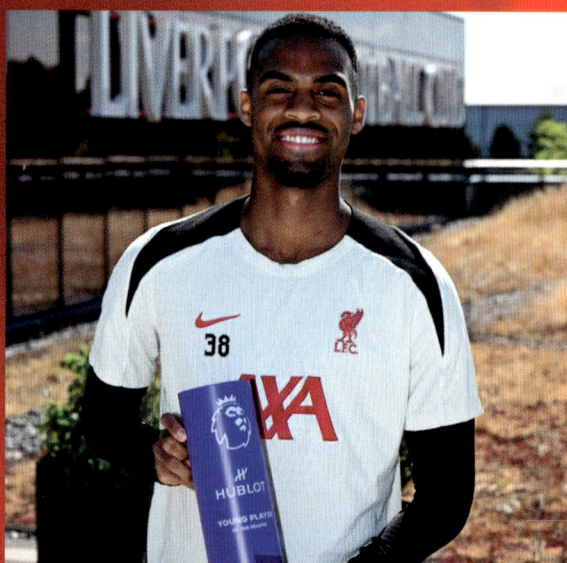

2024/25 FINAL TABLE

		P	W	D	L	GF	GA	GD	PTS
C	LIVERPOOL	38	25	9	4	86	41	45	84
2	ARSENAL	38	20	14	4	69	34	+35	74
3	MANCHESTER CITY	38	21	8	9	72	44	+28	71
4	CHELSEA	38	20	9	9	64	43	+21	69
5	NEWCASTLE UNITED	38	20	6	12	68	47	+21	66
6	ASTON VILLA	38	19	9	10	58	51	+7	66
7	NOTTINGHAM FOREST	38	19	8	11	58	46	+12	65
8	BRIGHTON AND HOVE ALBION	38	16	13	9	66	59	+7	61
9	AFC BOURNEMOUTH	38	15	11	12	58	46	+12	56
10	BRENTFORD	38	16	8	14	66	57	+9	56
11	FULHAM	38	15	9	14	54	54	0	54
12	CRYSTAL PALACE	38	13	14	11	51	51	0	53
13	EVERTON	38	11	15	12	42	44	-2	48
14	WEST HAM UNITED	38	11	10	17	46	62	-16	43
15	MANCHESTER UNITED	38	11	9	18	44	54	-10	42
16	WOLVERHAMPTON WANDERERS	38	12	6	20	54	69	-15	42
17	TOTTENHAM HOTSPUR	38	11	5	22	64	65	-1	38
18	LEICESTER CITY	38	6	7	25	33	80	-47	25
19	IPSWICH TOWN	38	4	10	24	36	82	-46	22
20	SOUTHAMPTON	38	2	6	30	26	86	-60	12

LIVERPOOL FC MAJOR HONOURS

League Titles

20

1900/01, 1905/06, 1921/22, 1922/23, 1946/47, 1963/64, 1965/66, 1972/73, 1975/76, 1976/77, 1978/79, 1979/80, 1981/82, 1982/83, 1983/84, 1985/86, 1987/88, 1989/90, 2019/20, **2024/25**

European Cup/ UEFA Champions League

6

1976/77, 1977/78, 1980/81, 1983/84, 2004/05, 2018/19

FA Cups

8

1964/65, 1973/74, 1985/86, 1988/89, 1991/92, 2000/01, 2005/06, 2021/22

UEFA Cups

3

1972/73, 1975/76, 2000/01

League Cups

10

1980/81, 1981/82, 1982/83, 1983/84, 1994/95, 2000/01, 2002/03, 2011/12, 2021/22, 2023/24

UEFA Super Cups

4

1977/78, 2001/02, 2005/06, 2019/20

FIFA Club World Cup

1

2019

Premier League
Premier League
Premier League
Premier League
25